6.05

D. H. LAWRENCE'S AMERICAN JOURNEY

D. H. LAWRENCE'S AMERICAN JOURNEY

A Study in Literature and Myth

JAMES C. COWAN

Essay Index

1970
The Press of Case Western Reserve University
Cleveland/London

To Judy
for the passage
with dolphins

Acknowledgments

FOR THEIR VALUABLE COMMENTS on my work, I am grateful to Roger B. Salomon and Richard H. Fogle, who read the manuscript, and to Alphonse J. Fritz, who read an early version of the study. Throughout my work, I have benefited from Joseph Campbell's illuminating studies of myth. For the purposes of this study, I found *The Hero with a Thousand Faces* especially instructive. My greatest indebtedness, both personal and scholarly, is to my wife, Judith R. Cowan, M.D., a practicing psychiatrist, whose influence on my work is everywhere apparent. Her comments on neuroanatomy and on the structure and dynamics of the psyche were useful. Our discussions of the philosophical and psychological dimensions of alternative Freudian analytic and Jungian synthesist modes of perceiving the world were not only essential to the present study but productive also in an ongoing shared voyage of self-discovery.

I am also grateful to the University of Arkansas for a grant to pay fees for permission to quote from works protected by copyright as specified by Laurence Pollinger Ltd. (for the Estate of Frieda Lawrence Ravagli), The Viking Press, Inc., Princeton University Press, and George Allen and Unwin Ltd.

The following portions of this study have been previously published in different form:

The discussion of *Studies in Classic American Literature* in chapter two was published as "Lawrence's Romantic Values: *Studies in Classic American Literature*," *Ball State University Forum*, VIII (1967), 30–35.

Chapter three was published as "D. H. Lawrence's Quarrel with Christianity," *Literature and Theology*, University of Tulsa Department of English Monograph Series, No. 7 (1969), pp. 32–43.

The discussion of *The Princess* in chapter five was published as "D. H. Lawrence's *The Princess* as Ironic Romance," *Studies in Short*

Fiction (Newberry College, Newberry, South Carolina), IV (1967), 245–251.

Chapter seven was published as "The Symbolic Structure of *The Plumed Serpent*," *Tulane Studies in English*, XIV (1965), 75–96.

Permission to use quotations from works protected by copyright has been granted as follows:

Excerpts from *Apocalypse* by D. H. Lawrence (Copyright 1931 by the Estate of David Herbert Lawrence. All rights reserved). Reprinted by permission of The Viking Press, Inc., and Laurence Pollinger Ltd. (for the Estate of Frieda Lawrence Ravagli).

Excerpts from *The Collected Letters of D. H. Lawrence*, edited by Harry T. Moore (Copyright 1962 by Angelo Ravagli and C. Montague Weekley, Executors of the Estate of Frieda Lawrence Ravagli, 1932 by the Estate of D. H. Lawrence and 1934 by Frieda Lawrence, 1933, 1948, 1953, 1954 and each year 1956–1962 by Angelo Ravagli and C. Montague Weekley, Executors of the Estate of Frieda Lawrence Ravagli. All rights reserved). Reprinted by permission of The Viking Press, Inc., and Laurence Pollinger Ltd. (for the Estate of Frieda Lawrence Ravagli).

Excerpts from *The Complete Short Stories of D. H. Lawrence*, Vols. II and III (Copyright 1922 by Thomas Seltzer, Inc.; renewed 1950 by Frieda Lawrence. Copyright 1928 by Alfred A. Knopf, Inc.; renewed 1955 by Frieda Lawrence Ravagli. Copyright 1933 by the Estate of D. H. Lawrence; renewed 1961 by Angelo Ravagli and C. Montague Weekley, Executors of the Estate of Frieda Lawrence Ravagli. Copyright 1934 by Frieda Lawrence. All rights reserved); excerpts from "The Princess" and "The Last Laugh" reprinted by permission of Laurence Pollinger Ltd. (for the Estate of Frieda Lawrence Ravagli); excerpts from "The Woman Who Rode Away," "Smile," "The Border Line," and "Jimmy and the Desperate Woman" reprinted by permission of Alfred A. Knopf, Inc., and Laurence Pollinger Ltd. (for the Estate of Frieda Lawrence Ravagli).

Excerpts from *Fantasia of the Unconscious*, by D. H. Lawrence (Copyright 1922 by Thomas Seltzer, Inc.; renewed 1950 by Frieda Lawrence). Reprinted by permission of The Viking Press, Inc., and Laurence Pollinger Ltd. (for the Estate of Frieda Lawrence Ravagli).

Excerpts from *The Later D. H. Lawrence*, edited by William York Tindall (1952), and from the "Introduction" to this volume. Reprinted by permission of Alfred A. Knopf, Inc.

Excerpts from *The Letters of D. H. Lawrence*, edited by Aldous Huxley (Copyright 1932 by the Estate of D. H. Lawrence; renewed by

Angelo Ravagli and C. Montague Weekley, Executors of the Estate of Frieda Lawrence Ravagli). Reprinted by permission of The Viking Press, Inc., and Laurence Pollinger Ltd. (for the Estate of Frieda Lawrence Ravagli).

Excerpts from *Movements in European History,* by D. H. Lawrence (The Clarendon Press, 1921; illustrated edition, 1925). Reprinted by permission of the Oxford University Press.

Excerpts from *Phoenix: The Posthumous Papers of D. H. Lawrence,* edited by Edward D. McDonald (Copyright 1936 by Frieda Lawrence; renewed 1964 by the Estate of Frieda Lawrence Ravagli. All rights reserved). Reprinted by permission of The Viking Press, Inc., and Laurence Pollinger Ltd. (for the Estate of Frieda Lawrence Ravagli).

Excerpts from *Phoenix II: Uncollected, Unpublished and Other Prose Works by D. H. Lawrence,* edited by Warren Roberts and Harry T. Moore (All rights reserved). Reprinted by permission of The Viking Press, Inc., and Laurence Pollinger Ltd. (for the Estate of Frieda Lawrence Ravagli).

Excerpts from *The Plumed Serpent,* by D. H. Lawrence (Copyright 1926, 1951 by Alfred A. Knopf, Inc.; renewed 1954 by Frieda Lawrence Ravagli. All rights reserved). Reprinted by permission of Alfred A. Knopf, Inc., and Laurence Pollinger Ltd. (for the Estate of Frieda Lawrence Ravagli).

Excerpts from *Psychoanalysis and the Unconscious,* by D. H. Lawrence (Copyright 1921 by Thomas Seltzer, Inc.; renewed 1949 by Frieda Lawrence). Reprinted by permission of The Viking Press, Inc., and Laurence Pollinger Ltd. (for the Estate of Frieda Lawrence Ravagli).

Excerpts from *The Rainbow,* by D. H. Lawrence (Copyright 1915 by David Herbert Lawrence; renewed 1943 by Frieda Lawrence). Reprinted by permission of The Viking Press, Inc., and Laurence Pollinger Ltd. (for the Estate of Frieda Lawrence Ravagli).

Excerpts from *Sea and Sardinia,* by D. H. Lawrence (Copyright 1921 by Thomas Seltzer, Inc.; renewed 1949 by Frieda Lawrence). Reprinted by permission of The Viking Press, Inc., and Laurence Pollinger Ltd. (for the Estate of Frieda Lawrence Ravagli).

Excerpts from *The Short Novels of D. H. Lawrence,* Vol. II (Copyright 1925, 1928 by Alfred A. Knopf, Inc.; renewed 1953 by Frieda Lawrence Ravagli. All rights reserved). Reprinted by permission of Alfred A. Knopf, Inc., and Laurence Pollinger Ltd. (for the Estate of Frieda Lawrence Ravagli).

A NOTE ON THE QUOTATIONS FROM LAWRENCE'S WORK

Throughout this book, page numbers following quotations of Lawrence's works refer to the editions given in my "List of Works Cited." Wherever "The Phoenix Edition of D. H. Lawrence" (Melbourne, London, Toronto: William Heinemann Ltd., 1954–   ) and The Viking Press, Inc., Compass Book follow the same pagination, both editions are listed. *St. Mawr, The Man Who Died,* and *The Plumed Serpent* are cited only in "The Phoenix Edition." *Movements in European History* is cited in the Oxford University Press edition, 1925, and *Lady Chatterley's Lover* in the 1st Authorized Unexpurgated Edition of Grove Press, Inc., 1959. *Phoenix, Phoenix II,* and *Twilight in Italy* are cited in The Viking Press editions.

Lawrence's letters, cited only by date, are quoted from *The Collected Letters of D. H. Lawrence,* edited by Harry T. Moore (New York: The Viking Press, Inc., 1962) except, as noted, from *The Letters of D. H. Lawrence,* edited by Aldous Huxley (New York: The Viking Press, Inc., 1936).

Contents

D. H. LAWRENCE'S AMERICAN JOURNEY

CHAPTER ONE

The End of the Cycle

D. H. LAWRENCE came to New Mexico in response not merely to Mabel Dodge Sterne's written invitation of 5 November 1921 nor even to what the rich American dilettante later described rather luridly as her nocturnally willing him to come.[1] He came in fulfillment of his own role as artist of the post-Christian myth. His thirty-seventh birthday, 11 September 1922, on which he arrived in Taos, marked the beginning of an experience in which Lawrence sought the means to personal and artistic regeneration for himself and to religious, political, and cultural regeneration for society. Lawrence's pilgrimage to the promise of America follows the pattern of the quest of the hero of romance, a paradigm which becomes the dominant structural and thematic image in his fiction of the period. As Joseph Campbell describes the mythic pattern of this quest:

The standard path of the mythological adventure of the hero is a magnification of the formula represented in the rites of passage: *separation—initiation—return:* which might be named the nuclear unit of the monomyth.
   A hero ventures forth from the world of common day into a region of supernatural wonder: fabulous forces are there encountered and a decisive victory is won: the hero comes back from this mysterious adventure with the power to bestow boons on his fellow man.[2]

Lawrence's American journey, the most important of his many travels, was, though with more irony and ambiguity than the heroic analogy suggests, essentially a quest for the symbols and myths whereby what he regarded as the waste land of modern western civilization might be revived. The purpose of this study is to discover, by examining Lawrence's fiction written from his arrival in America to his departure for Europe on 22 September 1925, what his experience and work in New Mexico and Mexico contributed to his thematic and technical development as an artist.

1

THE GENESIS OF LAWRENCE'S CYCLIC THEORY
OF HISTORY

For Lawrence, the potential for reviving the waste land was to be found, in every area of life, in personal and public commitment to the values of romanticism, that is, of dynamic organicism rather than static mechanism. Lawrence's commitment to romantic values was formulated and presented expositorily in several ways in the period just before his American journey: in the growing conviction in his wartime letters that he must turn from the crumbling moral order of British civilization to the promise of the American continent; in the cyclic theory of history that emerges in *Movements in European History* (1921); in the post-Christian religious philosophy to which he gives symbolic form in *Twilight in Italy* (1916) and "The Crown" (1915); in the dynamic concept of psychic anatomy presented in *Psychoanalysis and the Unconscious* (1921) and *Fantasia of the Unconscious* (1922); and in the organic theory of literary art and criticism which underlies *Studies in Classic American Literature* (1923). A consideration of these several expressions of romanticism as a major concern in Lawrence's life and art will provide, I believe, the most advantageous perspective from which to view the primary materials growing out of his New World experience.

Though he was already working toward the idea in the history of the Brangwens, Lawrence's conception of history as an unremitting cycle of death and rebirth throughout successive phases of civilization is stated most directly in *Movements in European History*, the text he wrote for Oxford University Press shortly after the prosecution of *The Rainbow*. The genesis of Lawrence's cyclic theory per se coincides so exactly with his rejection of Europe as a static waste land and his turning to America as the embodiment of an unrealized organic potential that it is impossible to separate the two.

Early in 1915 Lawrence still hoped that Europe could be regenerated. In a letter to Lady Cynthia Asquith on "Sunday" (probably 31 January 1915) he applies the cyclic pattern of death and rebirth to his own spiritual state:

We have no history, since we saw you last. I feel as if I had less than no history—as if I had spent those five months in the tomb. And now, I feel very sick and corpse-cold, too newly risen to share yet with anybody . . . .
The War finished me: it was the spear through the side of all sorrows and hopes.

Now he feels hopeful again: "I couldn't tell you how fragile and tender this hope is—the new shoot of life." Nevertheless, Lawrence soon writes to Barbara Low (11 February 1915) full of plans to "revolutionise this system of life, that is based on outside things, money, property, & establish a system of life based on inside things. The war will come to an end, and then the Augean stables are to be cleansed." As Lawrence indicates in a letter to Bertrand Russell (19 March 1915), he did not expect this spiritual rebirth to come through Cambridge intellectuals: "How can so sick people rise up? They must die first." Rebirth would come through people who spoke in their "real voices"; but as Lawrence commented to Eleanor Farjeon, "Scarcely anybody lets you hear his real voice."[3] Lady Ottoline Morrell says that in the spring of 1915 "as the War went on the horror obsessed him more and more. He was . . . intensely English, and had a passionate desire for the regeneration and development of England. He had the same kind of reforming and prophetic spirit as Shelley had. . . ."[4] In this spirit Lawrence writes to Eleanor Farjeon (18 May 1915), "We *can* by the strength of our desires compel our destinies. Indeed our destiny lies in the strength of our desires." Lawrence's and the Murrys' paper, *The Signature*, was inaugurated in 1915 in an effort to "do something" toward the regeneration of England;[5] and it was to be read, as he wrote to Lady Asquith (5 September 1915), by "people who care about the real living truth of things."

Lawrence's first written mention of his impulse to go to America makes the venture sound like an escape to a place of refuge:[6] "I feel like knocking my head against the wall: or of running off to some unformed South American place where there is no thought of civilised effort," he wrote to Lady Asquith (16 August 1915). But Lawrence's more clearly formulated plan of the following autumn to emigrate to America was motivated, not by the suppression of *The Rainbow*, an opinion which Armin Arnold has disproved,[7] but by his growing conviction that Europe was at the end of a falling cycle and America still at the beginning of a rising cycle of civilization. Arnold cites as evidence Lawrence's letter to Harriet Monroe (26 October 1915), written eight days before the seizure of *The Rainbow*, announcing his plan to come to America:

Probably I am coming to America. Probably in a month's time, I shall be in New York. . . . I must see America: here the autumn of all life has set in, the fall: we are hardly more than the ghosts in the haze, we who stand

apart from the flux of death. I must see America. I think one can feel hope
there. I think that there the life comes up from the roots, crude but vital.
Here the whole tree of life is dying. It is like being dead: the underworld.
I must see America. I believe it is beginning, not ending. [Huxley edition]

But, characteristically, Lawrence still wavered. Only four days later
(30 October 1915) he writes to Lady Asquith:

If the war could but end this winter, we might rise to life again here in this
our world. If it sets in for another year, all is lost. . . .
  So I keep suspended the thought of going away. . . . If I go, I will go
to America. . . . But I hope not to go.

The motive behind Lawrence's gradually formed conviction that
he must turn from England to America is to be found in the mood
conveyed in the imagery of his letters. Throughout the period Lawrence's letters employ the organic metaphor—seasonal change, vegetation, water, the germ of being—to the same end: to relate England
to hopelessness, death, and the past, and America to hope, life, and
the future. An examination of a few passages from the letters of that
crucial autumn of 1915 will illustrate the genesis of his cyclic view
of history in his unwavering vision of the English waste land and his
hope for its regeneration.
  For Lawrence, the literal autumn of that year presaged the metaphorical winter of western civilization. As he writes to Lady Asquith
("Tuesday," probably 9 November 1915):

When I drive across this country, with autumn falling and rustling to pieces,
I am so sad, for my country, for this great wave of civilisation, 2000 years,
which is now collapsing, that it is hard to live. . . . the past, the great past,
crumbling down, breaking down, not under the force of the coming birds,
but under the weight of many exhausted yellow leaves, that drift over the
lawn, and over the pond, like the soldiers, passing away, into winter and
the darkness of winter—no, I can't bear it. For the winter stretches ahead,
where all vision is lost and all memory dies out.

This autumnal world was, to Lawrence, an organism blighted by
disease. Thus, he writes to Lady Asquith (3 August 1915):

It is this mass of unclean world that we have superimposed on the clean
world that we cannot bear. When I looked back, out of the clearness of the
open evening, at this Littlehampton dark and amorphous like an eruption on

the edge of the land, I was so sick I felt I could not come back: all these little amorphous houses like an eruption, a disease on the clean earth; and all of them full of such a diseased spirit, every landlady harping on her money. . . .

In the literal war of this diseased world, Lawrence saw the destruction of a cosmos. For all the poetry to come out of World War I, no poet evokes both the sensory and metaphysical experience of an air raid with such immediacy as Lawrence does in his letter to Lady Ottoline Morrell (9 September 1915):

Then we saw the Zeppelin above us, just ahead, amid a gleaming of clouds: high up, like a bright golden finger, quite small, among a fragile incandescence of clouds. And underneath it were splashes of fire as the shells fired from earth burst. Then there were flashes near the ground—and the shaking noise. It was like Milton—then there was war in heaven. But it was not angels. . . .
   I cannot get over it, that the moon is not queen of the sky by night, and the stars the lesser lights. . . .
   So it seems our cosmos has burst, burst at last, the stars and moon blown away, the envelope of the sky burst out, and a new cosmos appeared; with a long-ovate, gleaming central luminary, calm and drifting in a glow of light, like a new moon, with its light bursting in flashes on the earth, to burst away the earth also. So it is the end—our world is gone, and we are like dust in the air.

As Lawrence saw it, the "mental consciousness" of such thinkers as Bertrand Russell was, despite their conscientious protestations, an integral part of the war spirit. In this vein he writes to Russell (14 September 1915): "Your basic desire is the maximum desire of war, you are really the super-war-spirit. What you want is to jab and strike, like the soldier with the bayonet, saying 'This is for ultimate peace.'" For Lawrence, the war spirit was anti-life because it was anti-love. As he writes to Lady Asquith (2 November 1915):

The one quality of love is that it universalises the individual. . . . It is an extending in concentric waves over all people. . . . So that if I love, the love must beat upon my neighbours, till they too live in the spirit of love. . . . And how can this be, in war, when the spirit is against love?
   The spirit of war is, that I am a unit, a single entity that has no *intrinsic* reference to the rest: the reference is extrinsic, a question of living, not of *being*.

Before the spirit of love could emerge triumphant over the spirit of war, the shell of mental consciousness had to be smashed. Writing to the Scotch poet J. O. Meredith (2 November 1915), Lawrence explains:

I am bored by coherent thought. Its very coherence is a dead shell. But we must help the living impulse that is within the shell. The shell is being smashed.

Like you, in your poems, I believe an end is coming: the war, a plague, a fire, God knows what. But the end is taking place: the beginning of the end has set in, and the process won't be slow. . . .

One has oneself a fixed conscious entity, a self which one has to smash. We are all like tortoises who have to smash their shells and creep forth tender and overvulnerable, but alive.

Only by smashing this external shell could one experience intrinsic rather than merely extrinsic reality. Only then could one have the courage of life rather than merely the courage of death. As Lawrence writes to the young poet Robert Nichols (17 November 1915): "The courage of death is *no courage* any more: *the courage to die has become a vice.* Show me the courage to live, to live in spirit with the proud serene angels."

Although he already sensed the extrinsic mechanism at the heart of the American capitalist ethic, Lawrence again and again identifies the potential for new, intrinsic being with the American continent. For the whole autumn of 1915, and for a time thereafter, the idea of America dominates his letters: America as a place of refuge, America as the site of Lawrence's Utopian dream of Rananim. In reference to his never realized plan to establish Rananim on a citrus plantation belonging to the composer Frederick Delius, Lawrence explains to J. B. Pinker (6 November 1915): "I hope to be going away in about a fortnight's time: to America: there is a man who more or less offers us a cottage in Florida. . . . It is the end of my writing for England. I will try to change my public." And he tells Lady Asquith ("Tuesday," probably 9 November 1915): "My life is ended here. I must go as a seed that falls into new ground." In another letter to her (probably 16 November 1915), he adds: "I shall try to start a new school, a new germ of a new creation, there: I believe it exists there already." As he explains to Constance Garnett (17 November 1915): "I know America is bad, but I think it has a future. I think there is no future for England: only a decline and fall." In a letter to J. M. Murry and

Katherine Mansfield (25 November 1915), he elaborates on the dream of an earthly paradise:

If only we can get there and settle, then you will come, and we will live on no money at all. . . . If only it will all end up happily, like a song or a poem, and we live blithely by a big river, where there are fish, and in the forest behind wild turkeys and quails; there we make songs and poems and stories and dramas, in a Vale of Avalon, in the Hesperides, among the Loves.

And to S. S. Koteliansky, Lawrence writes from Cornwall (30 December 1915):

We got here tonight. . . . This is the first move to Florida. Here already one feels a good peace and a good silence, and freedom to love—and to create a new life. We must begin afresh—we must begin to create a life all together—unanimous.

Ironically, in the months to follow, Lawrence was never accused of such subversive ideas as these; he was accused only of being a German spy.

Throughout the coming months the idea of Europe as a waste land and America as the place of a possible new beginning continues to dominate Lawrence's letters. Sometimes, as in a letter to Catherine Carswell (20 December 1916), he expresses the idea in purely personal terms: ". . . I believe that England . . . is capable of not seeing anything but badness in me, for ever and ever. I believe America in my virgin soil: truly." More often, as in a letter to Waldo Frank (27 July 1917), he states it in terms of the cyclic view of history:

I believe America is the New World. Europe is a lost name, like Nineveh or Palenque. There is no more Europe, only a mass of ruins from the past.
    I shall come to America. I don't believe in Uncle Samdom, of course. But if the rainbow hangs in the heavens, it hangs over the western continent. I very very very much want to leave Europe, oh, to leave England for ever, and come over to America.

Not until seven years after first considering forsaking the European waste land to establish an American Rananim did Lawrence finally make his pilgrimage. Even then his journey was not to Florida but to New Mexico—and not, of course, to an earthly paradise "in a Vale of Avalon, in the Hesperides, among the Loves," but to "Mabeltown," in

Taos Valley, among assorted arty folk, Indians, and ordinary American Southwesterners.

MOVEMENTS IN EUROPEAN HISTORY

In the meanwhile, Lawrence's growing concern with cultural death and rebirth emerged in *Movements in European History*, his apocalyptic view of the history of western civilization. Vere H. Collins, impressed by Lawrence's knowledge of history, suggested he write the text; and C.R.L. Fletcher, the Oxford historian, read and approved it in manuscript.[8] In his introduction Lawrence explains his approach to his subject. Although history as a mere "register of facts" is no more, he objects to the two leading contemporary methods of historiography, the graphic and the scientific. Graphic history fails by attempting to re-create the personality of past ages: "Personality is local and temporal. . . . And each age proceeds to interpret every other age in terms of the current personality." On the other hand, Lawrence argues, "if graphic history is all heart, scientific history is all head." Its failure lies in its attempt to forge "a great chain of logically sequential events, cause and effect demonstrated down the whole range of time." Rather than really discovering causality, we merely abstract it after the fact: "The logical sequence does not exist until we have made it, and then it exists as a new piece of furniture of the human mind" (pp. x–xi).

Lawrence himself approaches the subject organically in terms of an unremitting cycle of death and rebirth. Morse Peckham's discussion on the use of history in nineteenth-century romanticism is instructive in understanding Lawrence's purpose. If the individual could understand himself only in terms of the experiences which had helped to shape his personality, then, the early romantic writers felt, man could be understood only in terms of his interaction with the world. This "interpretational tension from Subject to Object" was often designated by the word "Spirit": "Reality, therefore, is the history of Spirit. . . . The Enlightenment placed perceptions by putting them into the frame of unchanging nature; Romanticism places them by putting them into the frame of historical process. Reality is neither space nor time; it is the process of history."[9] Lawrence, rejecting both graphic and scientific historiography, proposes instead to show the "Spirit," the impersonal force of the past,

to give some impression of the great, surging movements which rose in the hearts of men in Europe, sweeping human beings together into one great concerted action, or sweeping them apart for ever on the tides of opposition. These are movements which have no deducible origin. They have no reasonable cause, though they are so great that we must call them impersonal. [pp. xi–xii]

For Lawrence, "history proper is a true art, not fictional, but nakedly veracious." Like all "true art," then, it will have a "myth-meaning," not merely a literal meaning as a record of facts. It will deal not only with effects but with essences, with the "unknown powers . . . . that well up inside the hearts of men," which are "the fountains and origins of human history." Such a "myth-meaning" will lie, not in the local and temporal truth of linear time, but in the universal truth of cyclic time. "Life makes its own great gestures, of which men are the substance. History repeats the gesture, so we live it once more, and are fulfilled in the past" (pp. xii–xiii).

In the closing paragraphs of *Movements in European History* Lawrence makes his cyclic theory explicit:

So the cycle of European history completes itself, phase by phase, from imperial Rome, through the mediaeval empire and papacy to the kings of the Renaissance period, on to the great commercial nations, the government by the industrial and commercial middle classes, and so to that last rule, that last oneness of the labouring people. [p. 344]

Characteristically, Lawrence insists that the cycle moves by a twofold motive: "the motive of peace and increase, and the motive of contest and martial triumph. As soon as the appetite for martial adventure and triumph in conflict is satisfied, the appetite for peace and increase manifests itself, and *vice versa*. It seems a law of life" (p. 344).

It would be a mistake to see in Lawrence's application to history of the romantic concept of organic death and rebirth any such fully developed system as the cyclic theory subsequently set forth by Arnold Toynbee. Even a casual comparison of the two in précis shows the philosophical superiority of Toynbee's more sophisticated formulation of the theory:

Briefly stated, the regular pattern of social disintegration is a schism of the disintegrating society into a recalcitrant proletariat and a less and less effectively dominant minority. The process of disintegration does not proceed evenly; it jolts along in alternating spasms of rout, rally, and rout. In the last rally but one, the dominant minority succeeds in temporarily arresting the society's lethal self-laceration by imposing on it the peace of a universal state. Within the framework of the dominant minority's universal state the proletariat creates a universal church, and after the next rout, in which the disintegrating civilization finally dissolves, the universal church may live on to become the chrysalis from which a new civilization eventually emerges.[10]

It is worth noting, however, that the last sentence of Toynbee's statement strikingly parallels what happens in Lawrence's most apocalyptic novel, *The Plumed Serpent*.

Toynbee comments that, though taken for granted by "the greatest Greek and Indian souls—by Aristotle, for instance, and by the Buddha," the cyclic theory, to most western minds, "would reduce history to a tale told by an idiot, signifying nothing." For Toynbee the meaning in this seemingly purposeless cycle is to be sought in supra-historical divinity: "While civilizations rise and fall and, in falling, give rise to others, some purposeful enterprise, higher than theirs, may all the time be making headway, and, in a divine plan, the learning that comes through the suffering caused by the failures of civilizations may be the sovereign means of progress."[11] For Lawrence, at least when he wrote *Movements in European History* and for a time thereafter, this purpose was to be fulfilled in the figure of the strong leader:

A great united Europe of productive working-people, all materially equal, will never be able to continue and remain firm unless it unites also round one great chosen figure, some hero who can lead a great war, as well as administer a wide peace. It all depends on the will of the people. But the will of the people must concentrate in one figure, who is also supreme over the will of the people. He must be chosen, but at the same time responsible to God alone. [p. 344]

The Nietzschean properties of this figure—especially as Lawrence explores the theme of the purposeful strong man in the three "leadership" novels, *Aaron's Rod* (1922), *Kangaroo* (1923), and *The Plumed Serpent* (1926)—have been widely noted, sometimes with alarm by post-World War II critics. But Lawrence's phrasing is reminiscent less of Hitler than of Milton: "I call therefore a complete and generous education that which fits a man to perform justly, skilfully, and magnanimously all the offices, both private and public, of peace and war." Although Lawrence would certainly disagree with Milton on how "to know God aright," he would not quarrel with Milton's thesis, in "Of Education," that "the end then of learning is to repair the ruins of our first parents. . . ." For Lawrence, this means restoring the prelapsarian condition of animal innocence in which Adam and Eve had lived together before the Fall: "It didn't become 'sin' till the knowledge-poison entered." The contrast between the prelapsarian and the lapsarian conditions lay in modes of knowing: "Adam knew Eve as a wild animal knows its mate, momentaneously but vitally, in blood-knowledge. . . . all the vast vital flux of knowing that goes on in the dark, antecedent to the mind" (*Studies in Classic American Literature*, p. 94). Renewal of blood-knowledge was essential to the rebirth of western civilization. Rananim presupposed the possibility of restoring the prelapsarian condition. Lawrence's journey to America was a quest for the symbols and myths by which it might be done. The dominant, heroic figure, viewed from this perspective at a juncture in history marking the end of one cycle and the beginning of another, was a possible means to bring about the growth of a dynamic order of organic wholeness out of the ashes of the discredited static order of mechanistic fragmentation. But the question is not settled. Prophetically Lawrence concludes his study of history: "Here is a problem of which a stormy future will have to evolve the solution" (p. 344).

NOTES

1. Mabel Dodge Luhan, *Lorenzo in Taos* (New York: Alfred A. Knopf, 1932), p. 35.

2. Joseph Campbell, *The Hero with a Thousand Faces*, The Bollingen Series XVII (New York: Pantheon Books, Inc., 1949), p. 30.

3. Edward Nehls, ed., *D. H. Lawrence: A Composite Biography*, 3 vols. (Madison: University of Wisconsin Press, 1957–1959), I, 295.

4. Ibid., p. 308.

5. D. H. Lawrence, "Note to 'The Crown,'" in *Phoenix II: Uncollected, Unpublished, and Other Prose Works by D. H. Lawrence*, ed. Warren Roberts and Harry T. Moore (New York: The Viking Press, 1968), p. 364.

6. Hence, Armin Arnold entitles his second chapter "America as Place of Refuge (1914–1918)," in *D. H. Lawrence and America* (New York: Philosophical Library, Inc., 1959).

7. Ibid., p. 24.

8. Nehls, I, 471.

9. "The Dilemma of a Century: The Four Stages of Romanticism," in

Romanticism: The Culture of the Nineteenth Century (New York: George Braziller, 1965), p. 24.

10. *Civilization on Trial* (New York: Oxford University Press, 1948), p. 13.

11. Ibid., pp. 14–15.

CHAPTER TWO

Lawrence's Romantic Values

IF EUROPE had reached the end of a falling cycle, America was still at the beginning of a rising cycle of history. Lawrence wished not only to identify himself with that rising cycle but also in part to direct it. Eugene Goodheart ably elaborates the point that in Lawrence's work there is always "the ulterior view of the future." Calling Lawrence a Nietzschean "tablet-breaker," a figure who appears "at significant crises in culture and whose characteristic impulse is to divert the current of tradition into new and hitherto unknown channels," Goodheart says:

It is characteristic for the tablet-breaker to assume at various times the roles of nihilist, mystic, diabolist, and obscurantist, for the language of traditional thought and feeling would only give the lie to his grasp of the future. His refusal to assume traditional moral attitudes is not a refusal to be moral. On the contrary, the tablet-breaker has discovered immorality in the old attitudes, and, by assuming on occasion the mask of the immoralist, he attempts to express a new morality.[1]

With the English waste land behind him, Lawrence turned his gaze upon the American desert. As he quickly discovered, if a new morality was to be expressed in America, the American consciousness would have to be diverted from the mechanical will and redirected toward organic feeling. From the moment of his arrival in San Francisco on 4 September 1922, Lawrence found America a strange mixture of generosity and self-indulgence. If, as he indicated in a letter to Frieda's mother, Frau Baronin von Richthofen (5 September 1922), he was charmed by Mabel Dodge Sterne's telegram: "Mabel says: 'From San Francisco you are my guests, so I send you the railway ticket'—so American!," he also regarded American life with distrust: "All is comfortable, comfortable, comfortable—I really hate this me-

13

chanical comfort." The undependability of the foundation of America's industrial civilization was impressed upon Lawrence almost immediately after he alighted from the train in Lamy station. On the drive to Santa Fe the car stopped in the road. When Tony Luhan was unable to get it started, Frieda suggested that Lawrence get out and help. According to Mrs. Luhan, Lawrence retorted angrily: "You know I don't know anything about automobiles, Frieda! I *hate* them! Nasty, unintelligent, unreliable things!"[2] Lawrence records his first impression of America in a letter to S. S. Koteliansky (18 September 1922): "America is more or less as I expected: shove or be shoved. But still it has a bigness, a sense of space, and a certain sense of rough freedom which I like." Despite his reservations, perhaps because of them, Lawrence still had the reforming spirit, for, as he writes to Rachel Annand Taylor (21 September 1922), "deaths leave me only more aggressive."

Throughout his first autumn in America Lawrence moves, as revealed in his letters, toward a redefinition of the American ideals of freedom and bravery by a shift in consciousness from will to feeling. As he writes to E. H. Brewster (22 September 1922), American life "is just life outside, and the outside of life." But his impression of America at that point was based on his relationship with Mrs. Sterne:

The drawback is, of course, living under the wing of the *"padrona."* She is generous and nice—but still, I don't feel free. . . . What you dislike in America seems to me really dislikeable: everybody seems to be trying to enforce his, or her, *will,* and trying to see how much the other person or persons will let themselves be overcome. Of course the *will* is benevolent, kind, and all that, but none the less it is other people's will being put on me like a pressure.

The American woman, modishly free of external restraints, lacked the meaningful freedom to love. As Lawrence puts it in a letter to Harriet Monroe (23 September 1922):

I should say, wouldn't you, the most unwilling woman in the world is Thais: far more unwilling than Cassandra. The one woman who never gives herself is your free woman, who is always giving herself. America affects me like that.

The philosophical task confronting Lawrence is clearly formulated in a letter to Frieda's sister, Else Jaffe (27 September 1922): "Well, here we are in the Land of the Free and the Home of the Brave. But both freedom and bravery need defining." As he elaborates the problem:

Everything in America goes by *will*. A great negative *will* seems to be turned against all spontaneous life—there seems to be no *feeling* at all— no genuine bowels of compassion and sympathy: all this gripped, iron, *benevolent* will, which in the end is diabolic. How can one write about it, save analytically?

Frieda, like you, always secretly hankered after America and its freedom: its very freedom *not* to feel. But now she is just beginning to taste the iron ugliness of what it means, to live by will *against* the spontaneous inner life, superimposing the individual egoistic will over the real genuine sacred life. . . . And that's why I think America is neither free nor brave, but a land of tight, iron-clanking little *wills*, everybody trying to put it over everybody else, and a land of men absolutely devoid of the real courage of trust, trust in life's sacred spontaneity. They can't trust life until they can *control* it.

With rare insight Lawrence recognizes in his own nature the same contradiction that he sees at the heart of American experience, a dichotomy between will and feeling, surface sensation and inner being, extrinsic and intrinsic reality. In a letter to Catherine Carswell (29 September 1922), he says:

Perhaps it is necessary for me to try these places. . . . It only excites the outside of me. The inside it leaves more isolated and stoic than ever. . . . It is all a form of running away from oneself and the great problem: all this wild west and the strange Australia.

An American Rananim still comes to mind occasionally as a possible means of solving both personal and societal problems. To Bessie Freeman, Lawrence sends the invitation (on "Tuesday," probably 31 October 1922): "Then come, and let us plan a new life. . . . And the rule would be, no *servants:* we'd all work our own work. No highbrows and weariness of stunts. We might make a central farm. Make it all real." In a letter to Frieda's mother (5 December 1922), Lawrence perceptively links America's money lust to the anal drive for power: "If one would only say: 'America, your money is shit, go and shit [no?] more'—then America would be nothing."

PSYCHOANALYSIS AND THE UNCONSCIOUS and FANTASIA OF THE UNCONSCIOUS

Lawrence's comments on America and Americans, like many of his fictional characterizations, reflect the theory of human psychology which emerged from the fiction of the preceding period and which he elaborated most fully in the two essays on the unconscious, *Psychoanalysis and the Unconscious* (1921) and its sequel, *Fantasia of the Unconscious* (1922), which Lawrence wrote, in part, in rebuttal to the adverse criticism of the first essay. As Francis Fergusson has observed, Lawrence's gift was not for system-building but for "voice, *daimon*, inspiration, sensibility": "Lawrence had many visions, but no consistent doctrine."[3] Lawrence himself writes in the foreword to *Fantasia*: "I am not a scientist. I am an amateur of amateurs. As one of my critics said, you either believe or you don't" (p. 53). Logical consistency is not one of Lawrence's virtues. In *Psychoanalysis*, for example, he states: "We profess no scientific exactitude . . . ," but seven pages later he proclaims: "It is obvious, demonstrable scientific fact, to be verified under the microscope and within the human psyche, subjectively and objectively, both. . . . We can quite tangibly deal with the human unconscious" (p. 43). Lawrence's affirmation of the irrational, in both the form and the content of the two essays, has led many critics to regard his psychological theory either as fraudulent nonsense or as an elaborate mechanism of defense against any genuine insight into his own personal conflicts.[4] Recently, however, Philip Rieff, in "The Therapeutic as Mythmaker: Lawrence's True Christian Philosophy," a chapter of his important study *The Triumph of the Therapeutic: Uses of Faith after Freud*,[5] has given serious and thorough treatment to Lawrence's psychological thought. Certainly, to dismiss the two essays as easily as the earlier critics did is to deprive oneself of the valuable psychological insights which Lawrence's theory affords if taken seriously as a mythic restatement of ideas formulated artistically in the novels and poems.

Employing the cosmic image of the cross, Lawrence divides the human body into four psychic or dynamic centers. The vertical line bisecting the body divides the ventral sympathetic region from the dorsal voluntary region. The two dynamic centers of the sympathetic region are positive in polarity in that their function is to incorporate the other into the self. The two dynamic centers of the voluntary region are negative in polarity in that their function is to define the limits of the self in relation to the other. The horizontal line of the diaphragm divides the lower sensual plane from the upper spiritual plane. The sensual plane, with which Lawrence identifies the personality and culture of dark southern peoples, embodies the subjective unconscious in that the function of its centripetal gaze is identifying and relating to the self. The spiritual plane, with which Lawrence identifies the personality and culture of fair northern peoples, embodies the objective unconscious in that the function of its centrifugal gaze is identifying and relating to the other (pp. 34–35).

Lawrence makes no distinction between psychic and physical development in the human organism; indeed, the two are as irrevocably associated as in Freud's psychoanalytic theory or Sheldon's constitutional psychology. Differentiation of function in the four dynamic centers of "the first field of consciousness" begins, in fact, with the fertilized ovum: "The original nucleus, formed from the two parent nuclei at our conception, remains always primal and central, and is always the original fount and home of the first and supreme knowledge that *I am I*" (p. 75). This sympathetic knowledge is really that "*all is one in me*" (p. 79), since what Lawrence describes, with genuine psychological insight, is the infant's cosmic identification or, as Freud calls it, his "primary narcissism." As "primal affective centre" of the "pristine unconscious," the original nucleus remains "within the solar plexus of the nervous system." Though the infant "cannot perceive, much less conceive," it "knows" directly and vitally from the solar plexus. Likewise, in a creative "polarized vitalism," "from the passional nerve-centre of the solar plexus in the mother passes direct unspeakable effluence and intercommunication, sheer effluent contact with the palpitating nerve-centre in the belly of the child" (pp. 20–22). Wordsworth expresses a similar insight, without the paraphernalia of polarized dynamic centers, in *The Prelude:*

> . . . blest the Babe
> Nursed in his Mother's arms, who sinks to sleep,
> Rocked on his Mother's breast; who with his soul
> Drinks in the feelings of his Mother's eye!
> [Book II, ll. 234–237]

Characteristically, in an age that placed the unconscious, not beneath, but above, Wordsworth thinks breast and eye, not solar plexus, the centers of pre-verbal communication. In Lawrence's theory, the primacy of the solar plexus has physiological as well as psychological implications, for through this medium, he thinks, the infant incorporates the mother and the world in the act of nursing (p. 22). This assimilatory function of the Laurentian solar plexus strikingly parallels that of the Freudian oral phase of development, during which the self is not clearly differentiated from the environment and the infant gains knowledge by means of non-verbal experience, with the oral cavity as the primary means of assimilating the world.

The individuation process begins as the original nucleus divides: "This second nucleus, the nucleus born of recoil, is the nuclear origin of all the great nuclei of the voluntary system, which are the nuclei of assertive individualism. . . . In the adult human body the first nucleus of independence, first-born from the great original nucleus of our conception, lies always established in the lumbar ganglion" (p. 76). As the lumbar ganglion "negatively polarizes the solar plexus in the primal psychic activity," individuation begins with the child's ego differentiation from the mother: "There is a violent anti-maternal motion, anti-everything" (p. 23). From the lumbar ganglion arises "the first term of volitional knowledge: *I am myself, and these others are not as I am*—there is a world of difference" (p. 79). Instead of identifying cosmos with self, the infant now defines the limits of cosmos in relation to self. The child's "incipient mastery" is expressed in both playfulness and aggression. As a physiological corollary of this psychic rejection of the world, "the milk is urged away down the infant bowels . . ." (p. 76). This rejective function of the Laurentian lumbar ganglion is analogous to that of the Freudian anal phase of development, during which the sense of self as a separate, active being emerges as the development of anal control affords the infant his first opportunity to assert functions which are his alone.

Differentiation of function continues as the two nuclei split horizontally forming two new dynamic centers, which in the adult remain situated above the diaphragm. Paradoxically, the two nuclei below the diaphragm retain their original nature whereas those above have a new nature (p. 77). "The upper, dynamic-objective plane is complementary to the lower, dynamic-subjective" (p. 34). The cardiac plexus, which corresponds to the solar plexus in positive polarity and sympathetic function, does not, like the solar plexus, assert the dark knowledge that "I am I" as cosmic identity, assimilating the other into the self. Rather, it asserts the revelation in light that "you are you" as cosmic identity, merging the self into the other: "The wonder is without me. . . . The other being is now the great positive reality, I myself am as nothing" (p. 78). As a physiological corollary, the cardiac plexus controls the incorporative functions of eyes, heart, and lungs. The eyes, as in the self-effacing vision of the courtly lover, seek the ideal, unknown other in the outer world. Moreover, neither inhalation nor diastole is like the intake of food. "When we breathe in we aspire, we yearn towards the heaven of air and light. And when the heart dilates to draw in the stream of dark blood, it opens its arms as to a beloved" (p. 79).

On the upper plane, as on the lower, there is a counter movement as from the thoracic ganglion of the shoulders proceeds

a strong rejective force, a force which, pressing upon the object of atten-tion, in the mode of separation, succeeds in transferring to itself the im-pression of the object to which it has attended. This is the other half of devotional love—perfect *knowledge* of the beloved. [p. 37]

The thoracic ganglion, which corresponds to the lumbar ganglion in negative polarity and voluntary function, does not, like the lumbar ganglion, assert the subjective identity of the self in contradistinction from the other. Rather, it asserts the objective identity of the other in contradistinction from the self: "Objective knowledge is always of this kind—a knowledge based on unchangeable difference . . ." (p. 38). The thoracic ganglion, concomitantly, is the seat of power, of "the extravagance of spiritual *will*" by means of which one manipu-lates others as objects. Whereas the child's "rageous weeping," for example, derives from the lumbar ganglion, his crying to get attention derives from the thoracic ganglion. Similarly, the willful negativism of the upper center, as in the child's triumphantly dropping things out of sight over the side of his crib, is quite different from the in-dependence asserted from the lower center in such acts as his joyously smashing things. In balanced polarity with the other dynamic centers, however, the thoracic ganglion is the seat of constructive activity, "of real, eager curiosity, of the delightful desire to pick things to pieces, and the desire to put them together again, the desire to 'find out,' and the desire to invent . . ." (p. 80).

In Freudian theory, the functions of the Laurentian cardiac plexus and thoracic ganglion are paralleled by those of the phallic phase, during which the child, having emerged from the anal phase with a sense of self, struggles to understand realistically his position in rela-tion to the other. Like Lawrence, Freud sees the individual, during this phase of psychic development, as relating to the other ambiv-alently, alternating between unrealistic feelings of helplessness and omnipotence. In Freudian theory, as this ambivalence is resolved the individual enters the genital phase of development. Psychic maturity, characterized by realistic self-appraisal, is achieved; and the ability to give and take replaces the need to test.[6] In Lawrence's theory, a simi-lar maturity is attained in the proper balance of the four dynamic centers of the self in polarity with those of the other (pp. 44–46).

Whatever may be said for Lawrence's metaphors, his theory, if taken as literally as he sometimes states it, makes anatomical nonsense. Anatomically, the nervous system is composed of two broad divisions: the central nervous system, consisting of the brain and spinal cord, and the peripheral nervous system, consisting of the nerves which connect the central nervous system with the various body tissues. The peripheral nervous system, moreover, is composed of the voluntary nervous system, which mediates voluntary movements, and the autonomic, or, as it was called in Lawrence's day, the sympathetic, nervous system, which mediates involuntary functions such as caliber of blood vessels, glandular secretions, and the like. Only two of Lawrence's dynamic centers, the solar or celiac plexus and the cardiac plexus, can be located anatomically. There are no such single structures as *the* lumbar ganglion and *the* thoracic ganglion. The group structures, which are designated collectively as lumbar ganglia and thoracic ganglia, rather than assuming opposite functions from the plexuses, send their processes through these plexuses and have the same purpose of regulating functions of abdominal and thoracic viscera. All four of the structures which Lawrence proposes as primary affective centers are divisions of the automatic nervous system. Although he attributes to them such complex functions as integration, origin of impulses, and consciousness, in reality they merely transmit impulses which mediate relatively simple involuntary functions. The more complex functions of personality, as was known in Lawrence's day, arise in the great integrative systems of the central nervous system. Thus, in reifying his metaphor into literal fact, Lawrence burdens his four dynamic centers with more than these peripheral circuits can actually bear.[7]

Despite its anatomical errors, Lawrence's theory deserves to be taken seriously as a statement about psychic anatomy that is in the tradition of twentieth-century personality theory. Calvin S. Hall and Gardner Lindzey, in their authoritative study *Theories of Personality*, distinguish several modal qualities which are inherent in most theories of personality.

First, personality theory relies historically on clinical data and the creative reconstructions of the theorist rather than on experimental data and the values of the natural sciences. While Lawrence, of course, is more interested in his own hypotheses than in data of any kind, he adduces evidence which, loosely speaking, may be called clinical: his own perceptions of others; his own intuitive experience: "How do we know? We feel it, as we feel hunger or love or hate" (p. 20); his own creative work: "This pseudo-philosophy of mine—

'pollyanalytics,' as one of my respected critics might say—is deduced from the novels and poems, not the reverse" (p. 57).

Second, since personality theorists, historically, have been dissidents in both medicine and academic experimental science, personality theory has been relatively free from the kind of systematic and organized formulation that has characterized other scientific disciplines. Though when it suits his purpose, Lawrence dogmatically claims scientific validity, his airy dismissal of "scientific exactitude, particularly in terminology" (p. 36), and his flippancy about "pollyanalytics" reveal his pride in his own lack of academic discipline and systematic formulation. As he says in the foreword to *Fantasia:* "I am not a proper archaeologist nor an anthropologist nor an ethnologist. I am no 'scholar' of any sort." Though he has found hints and suggestions for his theory from ancient sources such as Herakleitos, Plato, the Yoga, and Saint John the Evangel to modern ones such as Frazer, Freud, and Frobenius, he declares, "I proceed by intuition" (p. 54).

Third, personality theory, "concerned with questions that make a difference in the adjustment of the organism," is functional in orientation. While therapeutic technique is not a concern in the two essays on the unconscious, Lawrence indicates, in his subsequent review of Trigant Burrow's *The Social Basis of Consciousness,* that he approves Burrow's group method of analysis:

The cure would consist in bringing about a state of honesty and a certain trust among a *group* of people. . . . So long as men are inwardly dominated by their own isolation, their own absoluteness, which after all is but a picture or an idea, nothing is possible but insanity more or less pronounced. Men must get back into *touch* . . . shatter that mirror in which we all live grimacing: and fall again into true relatedness. [*Phoenix,* p. 382]

The essence of morality, for Lawrence, is the true relationship: "the basic desire to preserve the perfect correspondence between the self and the object, to have no breach of integrity, nor yet any refaulture in the vitalistic interchange" (p. 28). Drawing his metaphor from electricity, Lawrence defines this relationship in terms of the four dynamic centers of the psyche: "Within the individual the polarity is fourfold. In a relation between two individuals the polarity is already eightfold" (p. 35). But Lawrence keeps the question "vital" rather than abstract because individual differences in both outer circumstances and inward need within the nuclear centers render impossible any real norm for human conduct (p. 85). The functional purpose of Lawrence's theory, ultimately, is to encourage the individual not so much *to know* as *to be* himself.

Fourth, personality theory customarily assigns the motivational process a decisive role. Lawrence rejects Freud's sexual motive, without really understanding it, on the ground that "when Freud makes sex accountable for everything he as good as makes it accountable for nothing." Lawrence's own definition of sex is highly restrictive:

Sex means the being divided into male and female; and the magnetic desire or impulse which puts male apart from female, in a negative or sundering magnetism, but which also draws male and female together in a long and infinitely varied approach towards the critical act of coition. [p. 59]

In one sense, "all life works up to the one supreme moment of coition." For Lawrence, however, the primary motive for all human activity is essentially the religious or creative one: "the desire of the human male to build a world. . . . Not merely something useful. Something wonderful. . . . And the motivity of sex is subsidiary to this: often directly antagonistic" (pp. 60–61). Whereas the creative motive leads to psychic health, neurosis results from "idealism," "the motivizing of the great affective sources by means of ideas mentally derived," because idealism leads to "the death of all spontaneous, creative life, and the substituting of the mechanical principle" (p. 11).

Fifth, personality theory maintains the Gestaltist position "that *an adequate understanding of human behavior will evolve only from a study of the whole person*," not from the segmental study of fragments of behavior. Lawrence maintains that "knowledge is always a matter of whole experience, what St. Paul calls knowing in full, and never a matter of mental conception merely" (p. 15). Furthermore, "we must patiently determine the psychic manifestation at each centre, and . . . we must discover the psychic results of the interaction, the polarized interaction between the dynamic centres both within and without the individual" (p. 35). Thus, Lawrence's theory, like most personality theories, is what Hall and Lindzey call an integrative theory.

Finally, "the stiffening brush of logical positivism has spread more lightly" over personality theory than over traditional psychology.[8] As Horace B. English and Ava Champney English put it in their *Comprehensive Dictionary of Psychological and Psychoanalytical Terms*, positivism is rooted in Comte's philosophical position that "knowledge consists of observation of sensory phenomena and the classification of these data according to the doctrine of necessary succession, . . . co-existence, and resemblance," which led to "the doctrine that science is limited to observed fact and to what can be rigorously deduced from facts." English and English list several dichotomies which distinguish positivism as a position in psychology. Lawrence's theory of psychic anatomy, consistent with his romantic position in other areas, is informed by values which, except in one instance, are diametrically opposed to the values of logical positivism. Thus, one way of defining Lawrence's theoretical position in psychology is by contrast with the positivist position. In psychology, the positivist, believing that the whole is to be understood only by means of studying its components, approaches his subject through analysis and embraces a reductionist psychology such as Watsonian Behaviorism. Beginning with the simplest unit, the single neuron, he emphasizes the role of the peripheral nervous system and the influence of the environment on it and sees complex functions as the result of the combination of these simple units. The effect is a psychology which sees the individual as an organism reacting to external stimuli, as in the Pavlovian conditioned response. The anti-positivist, conversely, believing that the whole is not the sum of its parts but that the parts derive their properties from the whole, approaches his subject through synthesis and embraces a Gestalt psychology. Beginning with the total organism, he emphasizes the role of the central nervous system and sees inborn phenomena, such as instincts and primary drives, as key determinants of behavior. Complex functions, he believes, are a creative process, not to be explained as a mere summation of components. The effect is a psychology which sees the individual as acting upon internal motivation.[9]

A position more antithetical to Lawrence's than logical positivism is difficult to imagine. Of the "science" to which he wishes "intelligibly to open a way," Lawrence says: "I refer to the science which proceeds in terms of life and is established on data of living experience and of sure intuition. Call it subjective science if you like." And of the science which derives from logical positivism, he says:

Our objective science of modern knowledge concerns itself only with phenomena, and with phenomena as regarded in their cause-and-effect relationships. I have nothing to say against our science. It is perfect as far as it goes. But to regard it as exhausting the whole scope of human possibility in knowledge seems to me just puerile. [p. 54]

But consistency, as has been noted already, is not among Lawrence's virtues. The inconsistency of his embracing the anti-positivist position in everything except in his emphasis on structures of the peripheral nervous system results, it seems to me, from his reification of a metaphorical construct into literal, physical fact and from his ignorance or disregard of the actual facts of neuroanatomy. Taken metaphorically, however, in terms of the intuitive insights which it represents, Lawrence's theory of human psychology is a respectable formulation of the romanticism which informed his creative work as well as a valid contribution to the body of twentieth-century personality theory in psychology.

STUDIES IN CLASSIC AMERICAN LITERATURE

Lawrence's hope for the regeneration of the waste land of western civilization lay in his essentially romantic view of man, nature, and the cosmos. The modern world, in his view, was characterized by a division between will and feeling, mind and body, which resulted in modern man's living from the nerve-brain self, under the control of the upper centers of consciousness, and repressing the blood self, under the control of the lower centers. His hope for modern man, then, lay in the reconciliation, which for Lawrence meant the balancing and not the merging, of these opposites of his being.

D. H. Lawrence's work is frequently cited as an outstanding example of twentieth-century romanticism. Thus, Horace Gregory calls Lawrence "an heir of the Romantic tradition in English literature."[10] Herbert Lindenberger places Lawrence's fiction, not in the tradition of the novel of social relations, but in that of the symbolist novel, the romance: "It is a form concerned less with the individual's connection with other people than his relation to larger forces and, for that matter, to himself."[11] Kingsley Widmer, recognizing "Lawrence's negative ways to his affirmations," applies T. S. Eliot's term "counter-romanticism" to much of Lawrence's fiction.[12] William York Tindall summarizes the consensus:

In the war between imagination and science, poetry and fact, feeling and thinking, Lawrence took his stand not only with Coleridge but with Blake and Baudelaire. "The two ways of knowing," he said in what might be the manifesto of the romantic movement, "are knowing in ways of apartness, which is mental, rational and scientific, and knowing in terms of togetherness, which is religious and poetic." Only through the creative unconscious, he believed, can the dead universe of fact come alive again.[13]

The critical values behind Lawrence's literary practice are clearly
set forth in *Studies in Classic American Literature,* the essays which
Lawrence wrote and revised in three distinct versions between 1917
and 1923. Of the twelve essays of the original version, which Lawrence wrote in Cornwall in 1917–1918, eight were published in successive issues of the *English Review* from November 1918 to June
1919. Of the second version, Lawrence's revision in Sicily in 1920, only
the essay on Whitman was published, in *The Nation and The Athe-
naeum* for 23 July 1921. The third version, Lawrence's revision in
America in the winter of 1922–1923, was published in book form in
New York in August 1923 and in London in June 1924. The extant
essays of the first two versions have been collected and edited by
Armin Arnold, with an excellent comparison of all three versions in
the introduction, under the title *The Symbolic Meaning: The Uncollected Versions of Studies in Classic American Literature* (1964).
Only the third version, the one familiar to most readers, will be employed in the present study.

If one accepts Morse Peckham's proposed definition of romanticism,
"the revolution of the European mind against thinking in terms of
static mechanism and the redirection of the mind to thinking in terms
of dynamic organicism," then Lawrence's critical theory is decidedly
romantic. In the radical terms in which Peckham distinguishes between them, the values of static mechanism and dynamic organicism
are opposites. Whereas the static metaphysic has the not mutually
exclusive values of changelessness and stasis, perfection and uniformity, rationality and the conscious mind, the dynamic metaphysic has
the not mutually exclusive values of change and growth, imperfection
and diversity, the creative imagination and the unconscious mind.[14]
Lawrence repeatedly affirms his partisanship for the dynamic metaphysic. In a letter to Lady Cynthia Asquith on 16 August 1915, for
example, he sees his quarrel with Bertrand Russell and Lady Ottoline
Morrell as a conflict between dynamism and staticism:

All that is dynamic in the world they convert to sensation, to the gratification
of what is static. They are static, static, static, they come, they say to me,
"You are wonderful, you are dynamic," then they filch my life for a sensation unto themselves, all my effort, which is my life, they betray, they are
like Judas: they turn it all to their own static selves, convert it into the
static nullity.

In *Studies in Classic American Literature,* which is itself a notable example of the expressive form, Lawrence specifically espouses the critical values of dynamic organicism and just as specifically rejects those of static mechanism.

Lawrence consistently approves temporal change, especially in the positive sense of growth. The process of growth, whether in the individual or in civilization, for Lawrence, involves the disintegration of all that is static and therefore decadent, and the reintegration of a new organic whole created in the deep passional center of man or cosmos. In the essay "Fenimore Cooper's Leatherstocking Novels," Lawrence discusses the reasons for the post-Renaissance emigration of Europeans to America:

They came to America for two reasons:
  1. To slough the old European consciousness completely.
  2. To grow a new skin underneath, a new form. This second is a hidden process. [p. 53]

And in the essay "Edgar Allan Poe," he applies this theory of growth to American literature:

. . . the rhythm of American art-activity is dual.
  1. A disintegration and sloughing of the old consciousness.
  2. The forming of a new consciousness underneath. [p. 65]

To the moralist's question "why Poe's 'morbid' tales need have been written," Lawrence replies, "They need to be written because old things need to die and disintegrate, because the old white psyche has to be gradually broken down before anything else can come to pass." But whereas in "true art," such as Fenimore Cooper's, "there is always the double rhythm of creating and destroying," "Poe has . . . only the disintegrative vibration" (p. 65).

Although growth, as a process of life, involves the deep passional centers, which Lawrence often symbolizes in primitive ritual, Lawrence does not, as some critics think, favor a return to primitivism. Change, as temporal progression, makes such a return, in fact, impossible. In his essay "Herman Melville's *Typee* and *Omoo*," Lawrence says that one cannot really relate to Melville's South Sea islanders. Though they are beautiful, childlike, and generous, they are, in a sense, uncreated in a far-off uncreated past: "Whatever else the South Sea Islander is, he is centuries and centuries behind us in the life struggle, the consciousness-struggle, the struggle of the soul into fulness" (pp. 136–137). The only permanent characteristic of life is flux, and even truth is subject to it. As Lawrence writes in the essay "The Spirit of Place," art tells the truth of the artist's day: "Truth lives from day to day, and the marvelous Plato of yesterday is chiefly bosh today" (p. 2).

Lawrence opposes perfectionist schemes—idealism, democracy, personal codes—because he sees in them exertions of conscious will, which he considers mechanistic. In the essay "Benjamin Franklin," as Armin Arnold suggests, Lawrence's purpose is to ridicule Franklin's belief in human perfectibility.[15] Lawrence satirizes Franklin's perfectionism by ridiculing (a) his pride: *"'That there is One God, who made all things.'* (But Benjamin made Him)" (p. 10); "The amusing part is the sort of humility it displays. 'Imitate Jesus and Socrates,' and mind you don't outshine either of these two" (p. 13); (b) his compulsive reification of living into a code: "He had the virtues in columns, and gave himself good and bad marks according as he thought his behaviour deserved" (p. 13); and (c) his emphasis on extrinsic rather than intrinsic reality: "Benjamin had no concern, really, with the immortal soul. He was too busy with social man" (p. 13). Lawrence also singles out what to him seem Franklin's perfectionist, and therefore not to be admired, activities of inventing "electrical appliances," becoming "the centre of a moralizing club in Philadelphia," writing Poor Richard's moralisms, being "the economic father of the United States," and approving extirpation of the Indians "to make room for the cultivators of the earth" (pp. 13–15). Lawrence finds some things to admire in Franklin—"his sturdy courage, . . . his sagacity, . . . his glimpsing into the thunders of electricity, . . . his common-sense humour"—but, he adds, "I do not like him" (pp. 13–14).

Essentially what Lawrence dislikes in Franklin is his manipulation of himself and others in static perfectionism rather than being himself and relating to others in dynamic communion. In his parody of Franklin's list of moral virtues, Lawrence seizes upon Franklin's verb "to use." Under "Chastity" Franklin had written: "Rarely use venery but for health and offspring, never to dulness, weakness, or the injury of your own or another's peace or reputation" (p. 12). The shift in values is apparent in Lawrence's correction:

Never "use" venery at all. Follow your passional impulse, if it be answered in the other being; but never have any motive in mind, neither off-spring nor health nor even pleasure, nor even service. Only know that "venery" is of the great gods. An offering-up of yourself to the very great gods, the dark ones, and nothing else. [p. 18]

Perfectionist schemes like Franklin's list of virtues were uniformitarian lies. The trouble with idealism, as Lawrence saw it, was that, like all intellectual productions, it falsified nature by trying to force its conformity to artificially formulated categories. In the essay "Hector St. John de Crèvecoeur," Lawrence charges that, as Franklin had arbitrarily categorized the human being, Crèvecoeur arbitrarily categorized nature: "Between them they wanted the whole scheme of things in their pockets, and the things themselves as well." Crèvecoeur's "Nature-sweet-and-pure business is only another effort at intellectualizing. Just an attempt to make all nature succumb to a few laws of the human mind" (pp. 25–26). In his essay "Fenimore Cooper's White Novels," Lawrence condemns the democratic, perfectionist ideal of equality: "When America set out to destroy Kings and Masters . . . it pushed a pin right through its own body . . . . the pin of democratic equality." Of the "intrinsically superior" Eve Effingham's democratic acceptance of the "naturally inferior" Septimus Dodge, Lawrence says: "Think how easy it would have been for her to say 'Go away!' or 'Leave me, varlet'—or 'Hence, base-born knave!'" Lawrence imagines a democratic encounter between Septimus Dodge and King Arthur, beginning with Dodge's "Hello, Arthur! Pleased to meet you," and ending with Dodge's taking over "that yard-and-a-half of Excalibur to play with" and prodding Arthur in the ribs with it. "The whole moral of democracy," Lawrence says, is that "superiority is a sword. Hand it over to Septimus, and you'll get it back between your ribs" (pp. 42–43).

In his essay "Hawthorne's *Blithedale Romance*," Lawrence derides the idealism of the Brook Farm experiment, though perhaps on one level he is recognizing the impracticability of Rananim, his own personal pantisocratic illusion. Such idealistic ventures, based on rationality, deny man's passional nature. They are doomed to failure because

you can't idealize hard work. Which is why America invents so many machines and contrivances of all sort: so that they need do no physical work.

And that's why the idealists left off brookfarming, and took to bookfarming. [p. 105]

In his essay "Herman Melville's *Typee* and *Omoo*," Lawrence condemns idealism as a mask for unrecognized evil:

No men are so evil to-day as the idealists: and no women half so evil as your earnest woman, who feels herself a power for good. . . . After a certain point, the ideal goes dead and rotten. . . . The whole Sermon on the Mount becomes a litany of white vice. [p. 142]

As for perfectionism in love, Lawrence feels that the static merger to which it leads causes a loss of individual integrity:

A "perfect" relationship ought *not* to be possible. Every relationship should have its absolute limits, its absolute reserves, essential to the singleness of the soul in each person. A truly perfect relationship is one in which each party leaves great tracts unknown in the other party. [p. 143]

Lawrence opposes uniformitarianism as counter to natural law and favors diversitarianism as central to that law. In keeping with the age of sociology and psychoanalytic psychology in which he lived, he usually thinks of uniformity as conformity, the loss of individual identity through merger with another or with the mass, and diversity as unique, idiosyncratic individuality. Thus, in the Poe essay he writes:

The central law of all organic life is that each organism is intrinsically isolate and single in itself. . . .
But the secondary law of all organic life is that each organism only lives through contact with other matter . . . with other life, which means assimilation of new vibrations, non-material. [p. 66]

But, Lawrence warns, "this glowing unison is only a temporary thing." The moment an organism's "isolation breaks down, and there comes an actual mixing and confusion, death sets in" (p. 66). In the essay "Whitman," whose undirected "I AM HE THAT ACHES WITH AMOROUS LOVE" and "ONE IDENTITY" themes Lawrence derides in several pages of exclamatory fragmentary sentences, Lawrence criticizes Whitman's confusion of sympathy with Jesus' love and Saint Paul's charity: "Sympathy means feeling with, not feeling for. He kept on having a passionate feeling *for* the Negro slave, or the prostitute, or the syphilitic. Which is merging" (pp. 173–174). The whole progression of merging is toward the death of individual integrity:

The merge into the womb. Woman.
And after that, the merge of comrades: man-for-man love.
And almost immediately with this, death, the merge of death. [p. 169]

Lawrence believes passionately in the creative originality which springs, not from rational, conscious mental knowledge, but from imaginative, unconscious blood knowledge. Peckham observes that the romantic concept of the unconscious mind "is really a postulate to the creative imagination," for "with God creating himself, with an imperfect but growing universe, with the constant intrusion of novelty into the world," and with reason inadequate to apprehend the truth, "the truth can only be apprehended intuitively, imaginatively, spontaneously, with the whole personality, from the deep sources of the fountains that are within."[16] For Lawrence, the "Holy Ghost" is the integrative force which prompts from within. As he says in the Poe essay: "It is the thing that prompts us to be real, not to push our own cravings too far . . . above all not to be too egotistic and wilful in our conscious self, but to change as the spirit inside us bids . . ." (p. 73). The consequences of Lawrence's romantic concept of the unconscious for both literature and criticism may be seen in his theory of "art-speech," which he explains in the essay "The Spirit of Place":

Art-speech is the only truth. An artist is usually a damned liar, but his art, if it be art, will tell you the truth of his day. . . .
    Truly art is a sort of subterfuge. . . .
    The artist usually sets out—or used to—to point a moral and adorn a tale. The tale, however, points the other way, as a rule. Two blankly opposing morals, the artist's and the tale's. Never trust the artist. Trust the tale. The proper function of the critic is to save the tale from the artist who created it. [p. 2]

Crèvecoeur, for example, "was an artist as well as a liar": "Crèvecoeur the idealist puts over us a lot of stuff about nature and the noble savage and the innocence of toil, etc., etc. Blarney! But Crèvecoeur the artist gives us glimpses of actual nature, not writ large" (p. 26). The fact that the tale speaks to the reader as unconscious to unconscious, whereas the artist speaks to him only as conscious mind to conscious mind, enables the artist to fulfill his function of making "myth-meaning." Although Lawrence does not suggest that everyone's fantasies are visions of universal significance, the artist, he believes, creates meaningful myth, not through the rational intention of his art, but through its irrational element of wish fulfillment. Lawrence says of Cooper: "His actual desire was to be: *Monsieur Fenimore Cooper, le grand écrivain americain.* His innermost wish was to be: Natty Bumppo" (p. 49). Thus, "*The Last of the Mohicans* is divided between real historical narrative and true 'romance.'" Lawrence prefers the romance: "It has a myth-meaning, whereas the narrative is chiefly record" (p. 58). The unconscious element in Cooper's work, like all true myth, "concerns itself centrally with the onward adventure of the integral soul" (pp. 62–63). When, as in Poe, the artist's unconscious has been perverted by will, the unconscious element in his work is concerned only with the disintegrative process: "All this underground vault business in Poe symbolizes that which takes place *beneath* the consciousness. On top, all is fair-spoken. Beneath, there is awful murderous extremity of burying alive" (p. 79).

Lawrence's reliance on the unconscious creative imagination is central to his position that, as he puts it in the Whitman essay,

the essential function of art is moral. Not aesthetic, not decorative, not pastime and recreation. But moral. The essential function of art is moral.

But a passionate, implicit morality, not didactic. A morality which changes the blood, rather than the mind. Changes the blood first. The mind follows later, in the wake. [p. 171]

Such a morality must take into account the duality of man. In the essay "Nathaniel Hawthorne and *The Scarlet Letter*," Lawrence elaborates:

Blood-consciousness overwhelms, obliterates, and annuls mind-consciousness.

Mind-consciousness extinguishes blood-consciousness, and consumes the blood.

We are all of us conscious in both ways. And the two ways are antagonistic in us.

They will always remain so.

That is our cross. [p. 85]

The moral change which it is the function of art to bring about is a balancing of these opposites to correct the imbalance between blood and brain, being and knowing, which at present exists in both civilization and the individual. The "sin" of modern society consists in the imbalance in favor of the "nerve-brain self." Lawrence postulates that before the apple episode Adam had lived with Eve as a wild animal with his mate. The diabolic undertone of *The Scarlet Letter* is that "man ate of the tree of knowledge, and became ashamed of himself": "It didn't become 'sin' till the knowledge-poison entered" (p. 84). The unforgivable sin against the Holy Ghost, in fact, is the failure to recognize and observe the limits of mind, will, and sensation. This is the sin of Poe's Ligeia, who, through exercise of will, turns life into knowing (p. 73). It is the sin of Melville's Ahab, a monomaniac of the idea, who hunts Moby Dick, "the deepest blood-being of the white race. . . . into the death of upper consciousness and the ideal will" (p. 160).

In Lawrence's religious but non-didactic morality, one's communion with the Holy Ghost is achieved by means of a reconciliation between mind and the pristine unconscious. Reverence for the dark gods lies at the heart of one's relation to others and to oneself. This is the meaning of Lawrence's serious parody of Franklin's creed:

"That I am I."
"That my soul is a dark forest."
"That my known self will never be more than a little clearing in the forest."
"That gods, strange gods, come forth from the forest into the clearing of my known self, and then go back."
"That I must have the courage to let them come and go."
"That I will never let mankind put anything over me, but that I will try always to recognize and submit to the gods in me and the gods in other men and women." [p. 16]

In Lawrence's expressive aesthetic, the artist, by means of this communion with the dark gods, avails himself of the creative sources of his art.

NOTES

1. *The Utopian Vision of D. H. Lawrence* (Chicago: University of Chicago Press, 1963), pp. 5–7.

2. *Lorenzo in Taos* (New York: Alfred A. Knopf, 1932), pp. 38–39.

3. "D. H. Lawrence's Sensibility," in *Critiques and Esssays on Modern Fiction, 1920–1951,* ed. John W. Aldridge (New York: The Ronald Press Co., 1952), p. 330.

4. See, e.g., Harry T. Moore, *D. H. Lawrence: His Life and Works,* rev. ed. (New York: Twayne Publishers, Inc., 1964), pp. 160–161; and William York Tindall, *D. H. Lawrence and Susan His Cow* (New York: Columbia University Press, 1939), pp. 39–40.

5. *The Triumph of the Therapeutic: Uses of Faith after Freud* (New York: Harper and Row, 1966), pp. 189–231. An earlier version of this chapter was published as "A Modern Mythmaker" in *Myth and Mythmaking,* ed. Henry A. Murray (New York: George Braziller, 1960), pp. 240–275. The

reader should also consult Rieff's introduction to the cited edition of Lawrence's essays on the unconscious as well as two earlier studies: Frederick J. Hoffman, "Lawrence's Quarrel with Freud," in *Freudianism and the Literary Mind*, 2d ed. rev. (Baton Rouge: Louisiana State University Press, 1957), pp. 151–176; and Eugene Goodheart, *The Utopian Vision of D. H. Lawrence*, pp. 103–115.

6. The Freudian theory of the stages of psychosexual development, to which I have referred analogously in discussing Lawrence's theory, is set forth concisely in Ruth L. Munroe, *Schools of Psychoanalytic Thought* (New York: The Dryden Press, Inc., 1956), pp. 178–211; and Calvin S. Hall, *A Primer of Freudian Psychology* (New York: The New American Library, Mentor Book Edition, 1957), pp. 103–113.

7. For a scientific exposition of the neuroanatomy with which Lawrence was concerned, as it was understood at the time he was developing his theory of psychic anatomy, see Henry Gray, *Anatomy of the Human Body*, ed. Warren H. Lewis, 20th ed. rev. (Philadelphia and New York: Lea and Febiger, 1918), pp. 701–721. In its various editions, Gray's *Anatomy* has been, for more than a century, a standard medical text.

8. My discussion of the modal qualities of modern personality theories is taken, with the indicated quotations, from Calvin S. Hall and Gardner Lindzey, *Theories of Personality* (New York: John Wiley and Sons, Inc., 1957), pp. 3–7.

9. The psychological terms of the foregoing discussion are defined authoritatively in Horace B. English and Ava Champney English, *A Comprehensive Dictionary of Psychological and Psychoanalytical Terms* (New York, London, and Toronto: Longmans, Green and Co., 1958).

10. *D. H. Lawrence: Pilgrim of the Apocalypse: A Critical Study* (New York: Grove Press, Inc., Evergreen Books Edition, 1957), p. xvi.

11. "Lawrence and the Romantic Tradition," in *A D. H. Lawrence Miscellany*, ed. Harry T. Moore (Carbondale, Ill.: Southern Illinois University Press, 1959), p. 326.

12. *The Art of Perversity: D. H. Lawrence's Shorter Fictions* (Seattle: University of Washington Press, 1962), p. viii.

13. "Introduction," *The Later D. H. Lawrence* (New York: Alfred A. Knopf, 1952), p. vii.

14. Morse Peckham, "Toward a Theory of Romanticism," *PMLA*, LXVI (March, 1951), 13–14. See also Morse Peckham, "Toward a Theory of Romanticism II: Reconsiderations," *Studies in Romanticism*, I (Autumn, 1961), 1–8.

15. *D. H. Lawrence and America* (New York: Philosophical Library, Inc., 1959), p. 45.

16. "Toward a Theory of Romanticism," p. 13.

CHAPTER THREE

Lawrence's Quarrel with Christianity

SINCE LAWRENCE'S American pilgrimage was, in essence, a religious quest, its nature may be understood best in the context of his quarrel with traditional western Christianity. When Paul Morel in *Sons and Lovers* takes his mother to visit the cathedral in Lincoln, the contrast between their responses foreshadows Lawrence's recurrent criticism of the modern church. Although "something in the eternal repose of the uplifted cathedral, blue and noble against the sky, was reflected in her, something of the fatality," Paul, sensing the negation of the life forces stirring within his adolescent consciousness, "all the time . . . was wanting to rage and smash things and cry" (pp. 240–241). If Paul's responses to the two other major female figures in his life reveal the Oedipal dichotomy with which the more important relationship with his mother has shackled him, they also reflect, in their contrast to each other, the two opposite modes of religious response available to him. Miriam Leivers, shy, intellectual, soulful, is spiritually possessive; Clara Dawes, outspoken, instinctual, passionate, is sexually aggressive. It is significant for Paul's maturation that he himself gains the strength to cut his external ties with all three women. He and his sister Annie collaborate in hastening the end of their mother's final illness, an action prefigured by their childhood sacrifice of Annie's doll Arabella.[1] The image of sacrificing the immature love-object also parallels the rites of sacrifice with which Paul terminates the other two relationships. Miriam he sacrifices physically in an unsatisfactory attempt at sexual union designed, perhaps unconsciously, to prove to himself the impossibility of such a relationship with her. Clara, in a similar reversal, he returns to her husband, to whom he sacrifices himself spiritually, first by relaxing his grip when he has

Baxter Dawes beaten in a fight and allowing himself to be kicked senseless, then by establishing a friendship with the other man during Dawes's illness.

The Oedipal components of Paul's relationships with all three women, and with Baxter Dawes, have been explicated fully enough to require no further comment here.[2] But it may be instructive to note that Paul can move in the direction of maturity at the end of the novel, walking "towards the faintly humming, glowing town, quickly" (p. 420), not only because he has begun the process of cutting the psychological bonds that still hold him to his mother but also because he has already rejected the halfness of experience represented by his relationships with both Miriam and Clara. In a religious sense, he has rejected two implicit offers of transfiguration: from Miriam the transfiguration of flesh into spirit, and from Clara the transfiguration of spirit into flesh. While it would be ingenuous to reduce Lawrence's characters to any simplistic formula, including this one, his heroes, from Paul Morel to the risen man of *The Man Who Died*, have the task of reconciling this duality of religious motive.

Nor can they expect any help from the church. Modern Christianity, in its reification of the spiritual motive into concrete, intellectualized "truth," which excludes the motive of flesh, actually operates against the sense of the holy by perverting worship, in T. S. Eliot's phrase in *The Hollow Men*, into "paralysed force, gesture without motion" (line 12). The problem of man today, as Joseph Campbell observes, is not the same as it was in the relatively stable time of "the great coordinating mythologies." Then meaning lay in the anonymous, cohesive group; today it lies in the self-expressive individual, but the meaning is unconscious:

The lines of communication between the conscious and the unconscious zones of the human psyche have all been cut, and we have been split in two.

The hero-deed to be wrought is not today what it was in the century of Galileo. Where then there was darkness, now there is light; but also, where light was, there now is darkness. The modern hero-deed must be that of questing to bring to light again the lost Atlantis of the co-ordinated soul.[3]

A church which, in the modern secular state, becomes merely the instrument of faction, of propaganda, and of self-congratulation may satisfy very well the chauvinistic requirement for a Sunday pantomime of weekday patriotism and business ethics; but it is hardly likely to help one coordinate spirit and flesh, conscious and unconscious into a self, far less to relate that self to others in a meaningful whole.

The cathedral chapter in *The Rainbow* provides a paradigm of Lawrence's quarrel with modern Christianity. Anna Brangwen teases her husband, Will, with the observation that the architect of Lincoln cathedral put his shrewish wife among the odd gargoyles carved in stone:

These sly little faces [Lawrence writes] peeped out of the grand tide of the cathedral like something that knew better. They knew quite well, these little imps that retorted on man's own illusion, that the cathedral was not absolute. They winked and leered, giving suggestion of the many things that had been left out of the great concept of the church. "However much there is inside here, there's a good deal they haven't got in," the little faces mocked. [p. 201]

Will, whose very name suggests his religious mode, has come to the cathedral to generate in himself a rather pompous, one-sided reverence for the awe-inspiring architecture. He insists vainly, "It's a man's face, no woman's at all—a monk's—clean shaven," but Anna's derisive *"pouf!"* of laughter signals his defeat:

His mouth was full of ash, his soul was furious. He hated her for having destroyed another of his vital illusions. Soon he would be stark, stark, without one place wherein to stand, without one belief in which to rest.
    Yet somewhere in him he responded more deeply to the sly little face that knew better, than he had done before to the perfect surge of his cathedral. [p. 202]

Yet Will Brangwen, the limited modern churchman whose religious practice is a kind of spiritual masturbation, lacks the genuine religious passion which enabled most of the saints to encompass the ambivalence of reality. It is the church *building* he cares for, Lawrence explains; and his passion is to manipulate stonework, woodwork, and organ to the end of self-satisfaction in a private ecstasy. The sacred myth no longer informs his worship with the sense of the numinous: "He was like a lover who knows he is betrayed, but who still loves, whose love is only the more intense. The church was false, but he served it the more attentively" (pp. 205–206). In his exercises of spiritual will, the modern Christian in his fatal division reduces religion to only a reified half-truth. Will Brangwen lacks the ironic, critical faculty which might have given him the psychological distance necessary to perceive the idolatry inherent in substituting form without grace for the wholeness of the Holy Ghost.

Lawrence's opposition to the modern church, of course, does not mean that he is irreligious. T. S. Eliot, who saw in Lawrence a culturally ignorant "medicine man" rather than an artist, nevertheless recognized, more clearly than many of Lawrence's favorable critics, that his response to the nightmare of the modern waste land was essentially religious: "He wanted a world in which religion would be real, not a world of church congresses and religious newspapers, not even a world in which religion could be *believed*, but a world in which religion would be something deeper than belief, in which life would be a kind of religious behaviourism."[4] Far from being irreligious, Lawrence, in the greater portion of his work, attempts to counter the staleness of a worn-out religious tradition with the vitality of a dynamic religious experience.

One of the means he employs, in the "On the Lago di Garda" chapters of *Twilight in Italy*, is a redefinition of the Christian Trinity. The duality of religious motive, in Lawrence's view, cannot be reconciled by compartmentalizing, but only by balancing, the opposing forces of dark and light within the self. Accordingly, the first and second persons of the Trinity are seen in the terms of a Blakean opposition between Tiger and Lamb, with the third person establishing the relation between the two. In a Laurentian version of the Hegelian synthesis, the thesis is "God the Father, the Begetter, the Author of all flesh" (p. 42); the antithesis is Christ the Son, the Celibate, from whom all spirit derives; and the synthesis, or rather its Laurentian counterpart, the relation of equilibrium and polarity established between the two, is "the Holy Ghost which relates the dual Infinites into One Whole, which relates and keeps distinct the dual natures of God" (pp. 58–59).

To elaborate, the way of God the Father, the way of Blake's Tiger, is the "way of transfiguration into the eternal flame, the transfiguration through ecstasy in the flesh." The first person of the Trinity becomes, then, within man, the ego of the first-person pronoun:

There is the I, always the I. And the mind is submerged, overcome. But the senses are superbly arrogant. The senses are the absolute, the god-like. For I can never have another man's senses. These are me, my senses absolutely me. And all that is can only come to me through my senses. So that all is me, and is administered unto me. The rest, that is not me, is nothing. . . . [p. 44]

The God within, like the tiger, is carnivorous, and his consummation is in "the supremacy of the flesh, which devours all, and becomes transfigured into a magnificent brindled flame, a burning bush indeed" (p. 44).

At the other extreme, the way of Christ the Son, the way of Blake's Lamb, is the complementary way of transfiguration into eternal air, the transfiguration through ecstasy in the spirit. The second person of the Trinity becomes, then, within man, the response to the other of the second-person pronoun: "God is in the others, who are not-me. In all the multitude of the others is God, and this is the great God, greater than the God which is Me. God is that which is Not-Me" (p. 48). Hence, the Beatitudes:

Blessed are the poor in spirit, for theirs is the kingdom of heaven. [Matthew 5:3]
    Blessed are they which are persecuted for righteousness' sake, for theirs is the kingdom of heaven. [Matthew 5:10]

Hence, also, the Commandments:

Whosoever shall smite thee on thy right cheek, turn to him the other also. [Matthew 5:39]
    Love your enemies, bless them that curse you, do good to them that hate you, and pray for them which despitefully use you, and persecute you. [Matthew 5:44]
    Be ye therefore perfect, even as your Father which is in heaven is perfect. [Matthew 5:48]

The Christ within, like "the lamb which the eagle swoops down upon, the dove taken by the hawk, the deer which the tiger devours" (p. 47), is the host to be eaten, and his consummation is in the supremacy of spirit, which sacrifices all and becomes transfigured into perfect abstraction.

Culturally, Lawrence consistently identifies God the Father with the civilization of dark, organically oriented southern peoples—with the sun-flooded Italians of *Twilight in Italy, The Lost Girl,* and "Sun," with the Mexicans and Indians of *Mornings in Mexico, The Plumed Serpent,* and *The Woman Who Rode Away.* The "secret of Italy's attraction for us," he declares in *Twilight in Italy,* is its "phallic worship": "To the Italian, the phallus is the symbol of individual creative immortality, to each man his own Godhead" (p. 56).

Culturally, Lawrence consistently identifies Christ the Son with the civilization of fair, mechanistically oriented northern peoples—with the English industrial magnates and society women of *Women in*

Love, *St. Mawr*, and *Lady Chatterley's Lover*. The English Puritans, he says in *Twilight in Italy*, established the negative orthodoxy of "the God which is Not-Me," concerning themselves not with the quest for salvation but with escape from damnation:

When they beheaded Charles the First, the king by Divine Right, they destroyed, symbolically, for ever, the supremacy of the Me who am the image of God, the me of the flesh, of the senses, Me, the tiger burning bright, me the king, the Lord, aristocrat, me who am divine because I am the body of God. [p. 49]

Even Alexander Pope's

> Know then thyself, presume not God to scan,
> The proper study of mankind is Man

is, for Lawrence, a proposition for greater abstraction, since the method of knowledge is not by instinctual experience, but by intellectual "analysis, which is the destruction, of the Self" (p. 49).

What Lawrence thinks of the northern Christian motive as an exclusive religious mode may be seen in his treatment in *Women in Love* of the industrial magnate Thomas Crich, who derives his financial reward from the coal mines he owns and his spiritual reward from keeping his colliers subservient to his will in the guise of Christian charity. For Mr. Crich, the other-directed Christian, the way to God is the way of identification with the other, of going the Second Commandment one better. Thus, he rationalizes his philanthropy as Christian humanism:

He had always the unacknowledged belief that it was his workmen, the miners, who held in their hands the means of salvation. To move nearer to God, he must move towards his miners, his life must gravitate towards theirs. They were, unconsciously, his idol, his God made manifest. In them he worshipped the highest, the great, sympathetic, mindless Godhead of humanity. [p. 207]

Thomas Crich's miners, however, experience his Christian charity as merely a paternalistic form of capitalist exploitation. His sense of spiritual reward seems almost to depend upon their humiliation and loss of dignity:

He was not deceived by the poor. He knew they came and sponged on him, and whined to him, the worst sort; the majority, luckily for him, were much too proud to ask for anything, much too independent to come knocking at his door. But in Beldover, as everywhere else, there were the whining, parasitic, foul human beings who come crawling after charity, and feeding on the living body of the public like lice. [p. 207]

Small wonder that Thomas Crich's allegorically named wife, Christiana, wants to set the dogs on the cringing supplicants and, in her husband's absence, has the servants drive them from the property and lock the gates. Smaller wonder still that when his son Gerald takes over management of the firm "the convulsion of death ran through the whole system," as Gerald, with that unfeeling, mechanical efficiency which characterizes the industrial waste land, systematically removes "the old grey managers, the old grey clerks, the doddering old pensioners" (p. 221) who have invested their lives in the company and replaces them with efficient young hustlers imbued with his own amorality, which Lawrence identifies with the death principle. It is poetically just, in view of the religious connotations of Lawrence's geographical and thermal symbolism, that Gerald Crich should freeze to death on an icy Alpine slope by "a half buried crucifix, a little Christ under a little sloping hood at the top of a pole" (p. 465).

Lawrence's thought, whether religious, philosophical, or psychological, is characterized by the world construct of opposites held in dialectical tension. The meaning of the world resides in neither side of the dialectic but in the dynamic polarity itself. Thus, in the essay "The Crown" (1915), the Lion embodies the qualities which Lawrence attributes to God the Father, the Unicorn those which he associates with Christ the Son, and the Crown the unity in opposition which he finds in the Holy Ghost. After quoting

> The Lion and the Unicorn
> Were fighting for the Crown,

Lawrence explains:

Thus we portray ourselves in the field of the royal arms. The whole history is the fight, the whole *raison d'être.* . . .
We have forgotten the Crown, which is the keystone of the fight. [*Phoenix II*, p. 366]

Lawrence's discussion makes clear that he has in mind a dynamic polarity between feminine and masculine, flesh and spirit, darkness and light, power and love—an opposition in which conquest of either side by the other would mean the end of creativity.

In religious terms, Lawrence identifies "the strength and glory of the Creator, who precedes Creation," with the darkness which "has nourished us": "a vast infinite, an origin, a Source." "This," he says, "is our God, Jehovah, Zeus, the Father of Heaven, this that has conceived and created us, in the beginning, and brought us to the fulness of our strength" (p. 368). In contrast, Lawrence identifies Christ the Son with the light, "the beam of chastity": " 'The End is universal light, the achieving again of infinite unblemished being, the infinite oneness of the Light, the escape from the infinite not-being of the darkness.' " In the creative conflict, first "the flesh develops in splendour and glory out of the prolific darkness, begotten by the light it develops to a great triumph till it dances in glory of itself. . . ." Then the light begins to detach itself from the darkness to become "the everlasting light, the Eternity that stretches forward for ever . . ." (p. 369):

Love and power, light and darkness, these are the temporary conquest of the one infinite by the other. In love, the Christian love, the End asserts itself supreme: in power, in strength like the lion's, the Beginning establishes itself unique. . . . It is the perfect opposition of dark and light that brindles the tiger with gold flame and dark flame. [p. 370]

In the conflict of "the two eternities fighting the fight of Creation, the light projecting itself into the darkness, the darkness enveloping herself within the embrace of light," reconciliation is to be found only in the balance of the opposition: "The lion and the unicorn are not fighting for the Crown. They are fighting beneath it. And the Crown is upon their fight" (p. 371).

In the terms of Lawrence's discussion of the same principle in *Twilight in Italy*:

The consummation of man is twofold, in the Self and in Selflessness. By great retrogression back to the source of darkness in me, the Self, deep in the senses, I arrive at the Original, Creative Infinite. By projection forth from myself, by the elimination of my absolute sensual self, I arrive at the Ultimate Infinite, Oneness in the Spirit. They are two Infinites, twofold approach to God. And man must know both. [p. 58]

Man must not, however, confuse the two: "They are always opposite, but there exists a relation between them. This is the Holy Ghost of the Christian Trinity" (p. 58). The unforgivable transgression against the Holy Ghost is, then, failing to maintain the proper balance between the dual natures of God, either by emphasizing only one to the exclusion of the other or by hopelessly merging and confusing the two.

Historically, Lawrence accepts the doctrine of Joachim of Flora, a thirteenth-century abbot, whose posthumous book *Introduction to the Everlasting Gospel* (published 1254) Lawrence cites in *Movements in European History:* "Judaism was the revelation of the Father: Christianity was the revelation of the Son: now men must prepare for the revelation of the Holy Ghost" (pp. 193–194). Lawrence imagines three epochs of man, the reign of the Father before the birth of Jesus, the reign of the Son from then to the present day, and the reign of the Holy Ghost yet to come.

The artistic and prophetic purpose of most of Lawrence's later work is, I believe, to usher in the epoch of the Holy Ghost. He cites Joachim of Flora's belief that "when the Holy Ghost began to reign the papacy and the priesthood would cease to exist" (p. 194). In Lawrence's later work, as in Walt Whitman's preface to the 1855 edition of *Leaves of Grass,* the departing priest is to be superseded by "the stalwart and wellshaped heir who approaches," who "shall be fittest for his days" in encompassing the ambivalence of nature and experience. The quest of the post-Christian hero, as Joseph Campbell says, is "to bring to light again the lost Atlantis of the co-ordinated soul."[5]

Thomas R. Whitaker, in "Lawrence's Western Path: 'Mornings in Mexico,'" one of the finest critical essays on Lawrence's American period, says that the travel book shows, in the strange image which Lawrence uses to discuss Melville's primitivism, that though we cannot take a stride back toward the savages, we "can take a great curve in their direction, onward." The arrangement of the sketches is, accordingly, designed to place "his various points of view as stages on a literary and quite unchronological journey":

The ego must descend to meet and accept what seems darkly inferior and destructive but is really its own unconscious life-source—projected upon a man, an animal, a people, or a landscape. If that acceptance occurs, if the marriage with the "other" or the "unconscious" is consummated, the closed and defensive ego may be transcended. A new self may step free, open to the creative flux beyond and within. Then only is true meeting possible.

As Whitaker demonstrates convincingly, the progress of Lawrence's tourist persona in *Mornings in Mexico* describes an arc of experience leading to such a meeting.[6]

In his insistence in his later work upon the spirit of place and the gods of place, Lawrence seems to affirm a pagan polytheism in contrast to Christianity's avowed monotheism. In what must have seemed to the average schoolboy reading *Movements in European History* an interpretation of Roman Christianity from the point of view of the lions, Lawrence pictures the Romans as at first puzzled, then irritated, and finally infuriated by the Christians' smug insistence upon theirs as the only god: "Why should not all gods be polite and respectful to one another . . . ?" "Why should this stubborn and fanatic people disturb the world in their hatred?" (p. 26). But if one hears, in the words of Lawrence's Romans, the Protestant voice of the most irritable of English non-conformists, one also discovers, if one goes beyond Lawrence's stated polytheism, a *syncretistic,* as opposed to *ethnic,* monotheism. As Joseph Campbell distinguishes between the two, syncretistic monotheism is "the inclusive, cosmopolitan, open, syncretic type," and ethnic monotheism is "the ethnic, closed, exclusive type."[7] Lawrence's polytheism is, in other words, a metaphor for an open religious system allowing multiple versions of deity, all representations in different cultures of the one unknown god of the unuttered name.

Lawrence's work in the American period is, in large part, the artistic record of his exploration of possible forms of deity of which modern man, as the inheritor of a burnt-out religious tradition, might avail himself in the interest of personal and religious regeneration. His subsequent work after his return to Europe, especially *Lady Chatterley's Lover,* "The Risen Lord," and *The Man Who Died,* is the artistic record of the result of this exploration.

NOTES

1. The point is made by William New in "Character as Symbol: Annie's Role in *Sons and Lovers," The D. H. Lawrence Review,* I (Spring, 1968), 34–35, 40.

2. See the discussions by Alfred Booth Kuttner, Frederick J. Hoffman, Daniel A. Weiss, and Frank O'Connor in E. W. Tedlock, Jr., ed., *D. H. Lawrence and "Sons and Lovers": Sources and Criticism* (New York: New York University Press, 1965), pp. 71–144.

3. Joseph Campbell, *The Hero with a Thousand Faces,* The Bollingen Series XVII (New York: Pantheon Books, Inc., 1949), p. 388.

4. *Revelation,* ed. Baille and Martin (London: Faber and Faber, 1937), pp. 30ff., as quoted in Father William Tiverton [Father Martin Jarrett-Kerr], *D. H. Lawrence and Human Existence* (London: Rockliff, 1951), p. 97.

5. *The Hero with a Thousand Faces*, p. 388.

6. *Criticism*, III (1961), 219–221.

7. *The Masks of God: Occidental Mythology* (New York: The Viking Press, 1964), p. 242.

CHAPTER FOUR

Lawrence and Murry: The Dark and the Light

FOR THE THREE YEARS between 11 September 1922 and 22 September 1925, Lawrence, except for a brief, eventful visit in Europe from 7 December 1923 to 5 March 1924, lived in New Mexico and Mexico. This period of near perfection in some of the minor work and significant, if imperfect, achievement in the major work produced the volume *St. Mawr* together with *The Princess* (published 1925), *The Plumed Serpent* (published 1926), and several stories, including the title story, in *The Woman Who Rode Away* (published 1928). In the following chapters, these works will be discussed in order of ascending significance, which is not to say quality, considering first the stories, then the short novel, and finally the novel.

Lawrence's long friendship and feud with John Middleton Murry provided materials for much of his fiction, including four of the stories in *The Woman Who Rode Away*. In all four Murry is cruelly punished: he is mercilessly ridiculed in "Smile" and "Jimmy and the Desperate Woman" and killed off in "The Border Line" and "The Last Laugh." The biographical materials of most immediate relevance to the genesis of these four stories are the events and feelings of the Lawrences' brief visit to England and the Continent in the fall and winter of 1923–1924.

MURRY, FRIEDA, AND LAWRENCE

Early in 1923 Murry wrote Lawrence of the death of Katherine Mansfield. Lawrence replied (2 February 1923) that her passing meant "something gone out of our lives," adding, "We will unite up again when I come to England. It has been a savage enough pilgrimage these last four years." The Lawrences left Del Monte Ranch for

45

Mexico on 18 March 1923 and remained until 9–10 July 1923, when they departed for New York for the first publication of *Studies in Classic American Literature*.¹ Lawrence wrote to Murry from New York (7 August 1923) telling him of Frieda's plan to go to England to see her children and asking him to "look after her a bit" because "wrong or not, I can't stomach the chasing of those Weekley children." On 18 August 1923 Frieda sailed. As she recalls in *"Not I But the Wind . . ."*:

> It was winter and I wasn't a bit happy alone there and was always cross when I had this longing for the children upon me; but there it was, though now I know he was right. They didn't want me any more, they were living their own lives.²

Lawrence, returning in the fall to Mexico with the Danish painter Kai Götzsche, found Chapala different without Frieda: " 'The life has changed somehow, has gone dead, you know, I feel I shan't live my life here.' " Götzsche wrote to Knud Merrild on 22 October 1923 that Lawrence was really "proud of England" and would return except for his "author ideas": "He wants to start that 'new life' away from money, lust and greediness, back to nature and seriousness."³

Meanwhile, unknown to Lawrence, Frieda and Murry, traveling together to Freiburg in September, 1923, had fallen in love. As Murry recalled years later in an entry in his journal dated 18 December 1955:

> On the journey we declared our love to each other. She was sweet and lovely, altogether adorable, and she wanted us to stay together in Freiburg for a few days anyhow, and I wanted it terribly. The idea of our sleeping together, waking in each other's arms, seemed like heaven on earth. I was worn out with the long strain of Katherine's illness, and Frieda's love was the promise of renewal. And Lawrence had been horrible to her in Mexico —something really had snapped between them. So I felt free to take Frieda, or thought I did; but when it came to the point, I didn't. I felt that, though he had treated me badly, still he had been my greatest friend (after Gordon let me down), and, at the very moment when the decision lay wholly with me, I said to F., "No, my darling, I mustn't let Lorenzo down—I can't." It was, I think, the one and only great renunciation I have made. And, I think, I'm glad I did. But it was a very *real* renunciation.⁴

Although neither Murry nor Frieda revealed the situation during their lifetimes, the story of their relationship, as it emerges in their ten-year correspondence from 1946 to 1956, published with Frieda's me-

oirs in 1961,[5] has the poignancy of youth remembered in age. In his
letter to Frieda on 27 May 1946 Murry recalls their moments together:
"Those moments of blessedness when I lay beside you fed something
in me that had been utterly starved. . . ." In her reply (4 June
1946), Frieda agrees that they were "fond of each other" and sees no
"blame" in that: "*Guilt* is stupid anyhow!" At sixty-six she does not
feel old, she says, "except peacefully": "I am sure Lawrence would
have been like we are now." Three months later (4 September 1946),
Murry writes: "What a queer young man I was, to be sure!" His one
redeeming quality had been a "capacity for love": "though may be it
was largely a desire for protection: for the safety and security of
love." His shrinking from betraying Lawrence, Murry admits, though
genuine, was an excuse for his own fear of love, which, for both men
and women, he still thinks of as "head-long self-surrender."

Five years later (9 December 1951), Murry is still obsessively justi-
fying himself: "You gave me something then that I needed terribly.
. . ." His wish not to be disloyal to Lawrence seems in retrospect
that Laurentian anathema "an 'idea'—something in my *head*." Though
it is unclear whom he includes, Murry has no doubt "that we could all
have lived together now happily and at peace." In her reply (19
December 1951), Frieda says that she, too, often thinks "of our friendship first and later of our intimacy with great satisfaction." On the
trip to Germany, she had been sad but not bitter because she had felt
that Murry was fond of her, and, "after all it was my job to see L.
through to the bitter end." She believes now that her "deepest feeling"
for Lawrence was "a profound compassion."

After seeing Murry briefly while visiting her children and grand-
children, Frieda writes (1 July 1952) to praise his book *Community
Farm:* "It isn't sentimental, thank God; in my old age I am sick of
emotions." Her visit with Murry had proved that "when people have
been real friends they don't become strangers, it was as if I had seen
you the day before!" A year later, Murry writes (20 July 1953) that
"not least because of you, I was able to love Mary"—Mary Gamble,
who became his fourth wife—with whom he has "complete physical
fulfillment": "I believe it would have been the same between me and
you, . . . if I had had the courage in 1923." He had not gone to New
Mexico, he finally discloses, because Brett was also going. He con-
fesses, "How bewildered I was—and still am—by Lorenzo's doctrine
of love-and-hate."

In a letter undated but written about the time of her seventy-fourth
birthday, Frieda agrees: "We shall never understand L.'s hatred. It

came like an impersonal, elemental thing out of nowhere and it frightened me, but a last scrap of me wasn't frightened. . . ." Lawrence's hatred, perhaps, was really love: "It exasperated him so much that people were so unfree and miserable." On 2 August 1953, Frieda recalls the circumstances of her first intimacy with Murry: "I think L. had become strange to me, when he came back and I was scared and your warmth was good to me and I was happy about it and deeply grateful." In a significant gloss on "The Border Line," however, Frieda states her belief that "there *is* marriage, you have it with Mary and I with Lawrence, that elemental, unconscious thing." And she asks, "Do you know that terrible story of L's *The Border Line?* The jealousy beyond the grave?" Frieda comments (29 August 1953) that whether "it was love or hate or both" between Lawrence and Murry, "the impact you had on each other was very real and very powerful." In his reply (24 September 1953), Murry agrees, but he thinks Lawrence's ideas on love both right and wrong: "The physical tenderness of love is just as much a spiritual thing as it is a physical." He had, for example, wanted *"all"* of Frieda: ". . . the generosity of your soul as much as the generosity of your body."

In a subsequent letter (undated, but written about Christmas, 1953), Frieda again recalls "that awful pity I felt for him, that I shall always feel, that he had to die and did not want to die." And returning to the theme of "The Border Line," she adds, "He still holds me, as if he said grimly, 'You are mine.'" Two years later (16 November 1955), Frieda tells Murry playfully: "For me you are always the old god Pan! You remember when Christianity came there was a voice heard crying: 'Pan is dead.' Maybe now Pan has come to life again." Murry replies (27 November 1955) with a comment on "The Last Laugh":

Funny you calling me Pan. Lorenzo, you remember, used Pan to kill me off in one of his stories—a queer one which I have never quite understood—all about me and Brett and a policeman in snowy Hampstead. Quite a good picture of me. Of course I understood that I was well and truly killed off. But I didn't and don't understand quite what, *in the story,* I was supposed to have done that deserved death at Pan's hands.

Frieda replies (10 December 1955) that she, too, dislikes and does not understand the story: "He really felt you as Pan and I fear envied you." Though Frieda and Murry apparently did not keep in touch after their brief intimacy, Frieda says: "Something ultimate and deeply satisfactory and new had happened to me; there it was, just an inner lovely fact, that I accepted without question for ever. . . . Lawrence was already very ill."

This is the period also of Lawrence's famous "Last Supper," a kind of shared vision—or delusion—which cast Lawrence as Christ and a number of his oldest friends as disciples, with Murry, of course, taking the role of Judas. The Lawrences gave a dinner at the Café Royal in London "for Lawrence's real friends," inviting Murry, Mark Gertler, S. S. Koteliansky, Mary Cannan, Dorothy Brett, and Catherine and Donald Carswell. During the increasingly tense meal, Koteliansky, who was already outraged at Donald Carswell for conversing with Lawrence in Spanish, a language the Russian considered Lawrence's "special perquisite," proclaimed that no woman, with the exception of Frieda, could understand Lawrence's greatness, an opinion which he punctuated by smashing wine glasses. In this emotionally charged atmosphere, the entire group of "normally abstemious" people drank a great deal of port wine. After dinner Lawrence asked each in turn to go back with him to New Mexico. As Mrs. Carswell expresses it: "Implicit in this question was the other. Did the search, the adventure, the pilgrimage for which he stood, mean enough to us for us to give up our own way of life and our own separate struggle with the world?"

Only Mary Cannan refused directly. Dorothy Brett made a simple and genuine commitment to go. The others, with unspoken reservations, promised to go. Then Murry went to Lawrence and kissed him, a demonstration which he said women could not understand. Mrs. Carswell recalls observing drily that "it wasn't a woman who betrayed Jesus with a kiss." At this, Murry embraced Lawrence again, saying, according to Mrs. Carswell, "In the past I *have* betrayed you. But never again," or, according to Murry, who seems to be quoting from Lawrence's letter to him of 28 January 1925, "I love you, Lorenzo, but I won't promise not to betray you." Whatever it was that Murry said, Lawrence soon fell sick and vomiting on the table. Miss Brett and Mrs. Carswell "ministered to him," as Donald Carswell, the soberest man present, was given the money to pay the bill. After Mrs. Cannan and Gertler departed, the others left in two taxicabs for Hampstead, where the Lawrences were staying. Mrs. Carswell's brother, awakened by the noise of Koteliansky and Murry carrying the unconscious Lawrence upstairs, later said that "when he saw clearly before him St. John and St. Peter (or maybe St. Thomas) bearing between them the limp figure of their Master, he could hardly believe he was not dreaming."[6]

There can be little doubt that Lawrence's reaction to Frieda's and

Murry's relationship, even if Murry did make a Jamesian renunciation of the affair so that Lawrence never realized its full extent, provided the immediate biographical impetus for the four anti-Murry stories of *The Woman Who Rode Away* volume. Whether these stories are valid satires on other than merely personal grounds remains to be considered.

"SMILE"

In "Smile," which has usually been dismissed as inconsequential, Matthew (Murry), husband of Ophelia (Katherine Mansfield), in answer to a telegram notifying him of his wife's critical condition, journeys to "the home of the blue sisters" where she is hospitalized, only to learn that she has died earlier in the afternoon. Although he has carefully primed himself for the role of "super-martyrdom," Matthew, on seeing his late wife's face, cannot suppress an involuntary smile. This inappropriate response proves infectious, for the three nuns accompanying him to the bedside cannot help smiling, too. Matthew, who has a kind of sexual fear of the Mother Superior and an alarming attraction to one of the other nuns, the dark one, eventually, though with some difficulty after seeing an answering mocking smile on the face of his dead wife, recovers his solemn demeanor as the Mother Superior seems to press toward him and makes his smileless escape.

Although the narrative itself is as slight as many readers have observed, the satire beneath the sardonic surface is serious. Employing the mock-heroic device of ludicrously overstating a trivial subject by comparing it to an exalted one, Lawrence compares the morally blind Matthew, in his melodramatic journey, directly to Christ on the Cross, "with the thick black eyebrows tilted in the dazed agony," and, by implication, to Orpheus, "walking in far-off Hades," and Hamlet, leaping agonized into the grave of his Ophelia (pp. 582–583). Lawrence cruelly exposes Matthew's lack of self-knowledge in the unconsciously determined smile, which undermines not merely Matthew's attempt to deceive the nuns with an expression of unfelt sorrow but also, more significantly, his wish to manipulate himself into the expected attitude of suffering.

Ambivalently mingling fear and attraction, Matthew's reaction to the three nuns is a projection of his characteristic response to women in general and to his dead wife in particular. The symbolic value of the three nuns as the triadic image of woman in man's life is made clear in Lawrence's subtle differentiation among the responses they make to Matthew's smile:

In the three faces, the same smile growing so differently, like three subtle flowers opening. In the pale young nun, it was almost pain, with a touch of mischievous ecstasy. But the dark Ligurian face of the watching sister, a mature, level-browed woman, curled with a pagan smile, slow, infinitely subtle in its archaic humour. . . .
   The Mother Superior, who had a large-featured face something like Matthew's own, tried hard not to smile. But he kept his humorous malevolent chin uplifted at her, and she lowered her face as the smile grew, grew and grew over her face. [p. 584]

As Theodor Reik proposes in reference to the three women in Offenbach's *Les Contes d'Hoffmann:*

Here are three women in one, or one woman in three shapes: the one who gives birth, the one who gives sexual gratification, the one who brings death. Here are the three aspects woman has in a man's life: the mother, the mistress, the annihilator.

Psychologically, Reik suggests, all such triadic constellations—Paris's three goddesses, Lear's three daughters, Hoffmann's three loves—have their source in a single figure, the mother: "She is the *femme fatale* in its most literal sense, because she brought us into the world, she taught us to love, and it is she upon whom we call in our last hour."[7] Mythically, the figure is not merely the mother but the Great Mother. As Robert Graves, who writes of her as the triple goddess, explains: "The New Moon is the white goddess of birth and growth; the Full Moon, the red goddess of love and battle; the Old Moon, the black goddess of death and divination."[8]
   Although "Smile" is, on one level, a rather tasteless psychological satire on Murry's personality, it also has a mythic level which gives structural and thematic coherence to what would otherwise be the pointless narrative most critics take it to be. On this level, the transposition of a symbolic value into its opposite, or the union of two opposites in the formation of a third principle, makes possible the equations of life with death, death with life, and sex with both. Thus, the paleness of the young nun identifies her with both the purity of youth and the decay of death. The Mother Superior's office and her facial resemblance to Matthew mark her as exactly what she is called, the "Mother Superior," the life bringer; but in her function of inform-

ing Matthew of Ophelia's death, symbolically a prefiguration of his own death, she is also the death bringer. The pagan maturity of the dark nun emphasizes her sexual potential, but the holy book she carries suggests also her funereal role. The metaphoric identification of the nuns' hands with birds throughout the story suggests not only the traditional religious association of birds with soul or spirit and thus with death but also the traditional folk association of birds with sex. The final merger of the three nuns into a single symbol of death comes as they move down the corridor "like dark swans down the river" (p. 586), the same image, incidentally, that Gian-Carlo Menotti uses as a symbol of death in the gypsy song that Monica sings at the end of Act I of *The Medium*.

The satire against Matthew turns only in part on his inability to maintain the level of bathos he wishes and on the involuntary smile which betrays his actual feeling. It turns in a deeper sense on Matthew's lack of self-awareness, a product of his unresolved ambivalence about all three aspects of woman.

"THE BORDER LINE"

"The Border Line," the first of Lawrence's sexual ghost stories, turns on the biographical and archetypal situation of the competition of two men, representing the opposites of light and dark, for the love of a woman at the border between life and death. Philip Farquhar (Murry), who marries Katherine (Frieda) after her first husband and his best friend, Alan Anstruther (Lawrence), has been killed in World War I, is superseded by the ghost of Alan, who, even in spirit form, asserts the inevitable superiority of Laurentian dominance in blood consciousness to Murryan manipulation in fawning weakness. The ghostly husband frees Katherine from Philip's clutch of death and takes her to bed as Philip dies.

The title of the story refers to the multiple border line between a series of paired opposites presented on various levels of abstraction —Alan and Philip, male and female, blood consciousness and sterility, life and death, reality and unreality—a line which is symbolized in the story by the Rhine, "that point of pure negation, where the two races neutralised one another, and no polarity was felt, no life—no principle dominated" (p. 599). Alan observes pointedly of Philip: "He's too much over the wrong side of the border for me" (p. 590). Alan, needless to say, is on the right side, and the plot of the story is concerned solely with Katherine's being made aware of that fact.

Katherine herself is described as a "queen-bee." She tips porters handsomely out of "a morbid fear of underpaying anyone, but particularly a man who was eager to serve her." "Secretly somewhere inside herself she felt that with her queen-bee love, and queen-bee will, she *could* divert the whole flow of history—nay, even reverse it." And when Alan is missing in action, she evolves from drone-killing queen to man-devouring earth mother: "The queen-bee has recovered her sway, as queen of the earth; the woman, the mother, the female with the ear of corn in her hand, as against the man with the sword" (pp. 587–591).

The two Englishmen Katherine marries are opposite extremes of character. Alan Anstruther, her first husband, is "that red-haired fighting Celt," the son of a Scottish baronet, and a captain in a Highland regiment, "handsome in uniform, with his kilt swinging and his blue eye glaring." A typical Laurentian hero, Alan has, even "stark naked, . . . a bony, dauntless overbearing manliness of his own." What Katherine cannot "quite appreciate" in him is his innate superiority: "his silent, indomitable assumption that he was actually first-born, a born lord." Philip Farquhar, Alan's hero-worshipping friend, does appreciate Alan's nobility. For him Alan becomes a touchstone of reality: "When a thing really touches Alan, it is tested once and for all. You know if it's false or not. He's the only man I ever met who *can't help* being real." Philip so strongly identifies himself with Alan as an ego ideal that he becomes Katherine's second husband. He does not, however, emulate Alan in the arts of war; to him the war is "monstrous," "a colossal, disgraceful accident." He spends the war as "a journalist, always throwing his weight on the side of humanity, and human truth and peace." Instead of Alan's aristocratic dominance, Philip has a "subtle, fawning power": "I'm different! My strength lies in giving in—and then recovering myself." Shortly after Katherine marries Philip, she is filled with "a curious sense of degradation": "Life became dull and unreal to her. . . ." She realizes, at last, "the difference between being married to a soldier, a ceaseless born fighter, a sword not to be sheathed, and this other man, this cunning civilian, this subtle equivocator, this adjuster of the scales of truth" (pp. 588–592).

At this point, Katherine, who is of German descent, makes her journey to the Rhine. Here, as Kingsley Widmer suggests, "the story turns from realism to allegory as the heroine undergoes an inverted religious experience" as she stares at a Gothic church, which she perceives as a "living and threatening 'Thing'":

There it was, in the upper darkness of the ponderous winter night, like a menace. She remembered her spirit used in the past to soar aloft with it. But now, looming with a faint rust of blood out of the upper black heavens, the Thing stood suspended, looking down with vast, demonish menace, calm and implacable.

Mystery and dim, ancient fear came over the woman's soul. The cathedral looked so strange and demonish-heathen. And an ancient, indomitable blood seemed to stir in it. It stood there like some vast silent beast with teeth of stone, waiting and wondering when to stoop against this pallid humanity.

And dimly she realised that behind all the ashy pallor and sulphur of our civilisation, lurks the great blood-creature waiting, implacable and eternal, ready at last to crush our white brittleness and let the shadowy blood move erect once more, in a new implacable pride and strength. Even out of the lower heavens looms the great blood-dusky Thing, blotting out the Cross it was supposed to exalt. [pp. 595–596]

For Widmer, who comments that "the Latinate rotundity stylizes the emotion of the apocalyptic vision," the passage recalls the "demonic attack on the sentimentalist and rationalist sensibility" which Melville, Yeats, and Faulkner make: "The blood and phallic beast of the second coming, the primordial urge in the blood, the demonic, heathenish black heaven, and the ancient fear of the implacable menace and mystery reveal essential aspects of the Christian tradition, only partly obscured by the Christian symbols of religious love."[9]

Immediately after Katherine's apocalyptic vision both husbands are re-introduced in terms of the allegorical valuations established for them in the description of the cathedral. Philip embodies metaphorically the "white brittleness" of "pallid humanity" to be crushed by the blood beast, whereas Alan, even in ghostly form, is the "shadowy blood" moving erect, the risen phallic principle of blood consciousness.

As Katherine turns from her vision she sees a man, "dark and motionless," and knows instinctively that it is the spirit of Alan, her "demon lover" (p. 596). The ghost, a kind of inverted Orpheus figure, conducts her to the bridge, symbolically to the border line of consciousness, and seemingly promises, with only the wave of his hand, never to leave her again.

When Katherine, as planned, meets Philip in Oos, he is obviously ill. Symbolically, Philip is "frightfully cold" and unable to get warm because "Germany freezes my inside, and does something to my chest" (p. 600). Derisively Katherine and her sister Marianne belittle Philip as "the little one" and the "stand-up-mannikin," terms expressing the same idea as the reference to Juliet's husband's "futile little penis" in the unexpurgated edition of "Sun." Philip responds to his worsening condition with manipulative "clinging dependence." In terms of Lawrence's theory of personality, Philip has the same affliction as Sir Clifford Chatterley, a symbolic modern disease whose symptoms may be described as atrophy of the solar plexus, lumbar ganglion, and thoracic ganglion, in a cardiac-plexus-oriented personality whose hypocritical, self-effacing mode of relating to the world proves insufficient to cope with the demonic heritage of Celtic darkness. In a typically graphic illustration Lawrence contrasts Philip's flaccidity and sterility with Alan's tumescence and fertility. Philip, "who never would walk firm on his legs," "just flopped," whereas Alan is identified with "a great round fir-trunk that stood so alive and potent, so physical, bristling all its vast drooping greenness above the snow" (p. 603).

In the final scene the ghost of Alan delivers Katherine from Philip's clinging dependence by loosening the literal hold of his hands from her neck. As Philip dies, his lips "unfurled" to show "his big teeth in a ghastly grin of death," which Lawrence, in what seems a pointed reference to Murry's relationship with Frieda, calls the "sickly grin of a thief caught in the very act," Alan makes love to Katherine in the other bed "in the silent passion of a husband come back from a very long journey" (p. 604).

Lawrence's technique in "The Border Line" is perhaps best summarized by one of his severest critics. Anthony West's view that "the characters have been taken much further as symbols than is usual with Lawrence" is correct: "Experience has been generalized nearly to the point of abstraction, and the characters are nearly as much ideas as flesh and blood people."[10] I would quarrel only with the implication that this tendency toward abstraction is a flaw. Lawrence achieved what he set out to achieve: a well-executed if minor tale in the genre of topical and moral allegory.

"JIMMY AND THE DESPERATE WOMAN"

In "Jimmy and the Desperate Woman" the typical Laurentian triangle ironically illustrates the title of an afternoon lecture by one of the men on *Men in Books and Men in Life*. In reference to Jimmy Frith (Murry), the effete littérateur and highbrow editor, Lawrence cannot resist the heavy sarcasm, "Naturally, men in Books came first" (p. 609). The figure for "men in life," of course, is Pinnegar (Lawrence), the sardonic miner. Emilia Pinnegar (Frieda) is, like many Laurentian female characters, modern woman in search of identity.

In the now familiar pattern Lawrence's man of light and intellect wins the woman, only to wonder, when he has her, what to do with her. The woman, in turn, discovers in herself a fidelity deeper than conscious awareness to the man of darkness and blood. Frith, needing "some woman's bosom" to fall on, sets out to find a "womanly woman," the sort who might even fall on his bosom instead. When Emilia, unhappily married to "a man who lives in the same house with me, but goes to another woman," submits to the editor a poem, "The Coal-Miner," "By His Wife," Frith is attracted by "something desperate in the woman, something tragic" (pp. 605–608). Arranging a meeting, he invites her, in an afternoon of romantic role playing, to come live with him, to bring her daughter Jane along, and even to marry him, should marriage prove to be what they want. When he hears the plan, Pinnegar observes drily, "You've caught a funny fish this time, with your poetry." As far as he is concerned his wife "has a blank cheque . . . to do as she likes." Emilia, who says she cannot come that day, promises abruptly, before Frith can collect his second thoughts, to come on Monday. In an ironic shift Frith becomes the desperate one when, unable to take responsibility even for his own reservations, he projects them on Emilia: "Don't come, please," he writes her, "unless you are absolutely sure of yourself." When she arrives on schedule, Frith sets his teeth and greets her with the false heartiness of "I'm *awfully* glad you came." For her part, Emilia is still, unconsciously and irrevocably, committed to Pinnegar, a bond which only makes her the more desirable to Frith (pp. 623–629).

The competition for the woman's soul as ultimate being centered in sexual commitment is worked out with the clarity and precision of a morality play. This is true of much of Lawrence's fiction, though, of course, each of the various sub-species of his fiction, ranging from almost pure allegory to psychological realism, moves on its own appropriate level of abstraction and generates its own appropriate tone. The tone of "Jimmy and the Desperate Woman," as determined by its satiric purpose, is comically ironic. Frith and Pinnegar, whose names are puns on "froth" and "vinegar," illustrate in their characters the values that Lawrence attaches to the properties of surface bubbling and acid in depth.

Frith, as a sexually ambiguous literary dilettante, is introspective without insight because he is concerned more with style than with substance, more with the figure he cuts in assuming his various roles than with genuine experience, more with book-likeness than with life-likeness. Though he has a misleading resemblance to Pan, Frith, ironically, sees himself as "a Martyred Saint Sebastian with the mind of a Plato," Lawrence's metaphor for the mentalized "Idea" in a passive, arrow-riddled body. Though Frith, concerned only academically with life, has "scarcely set foot north of Oxford," he now sets off, in a mock-heroic parallel, "like some modern Ulysses wandering in the realms of Hecate." He plays out his charade of courting Emilia in a parody of low-mimetic romance: "You ought to get away from here," he tells her. "Why don't you come and live with me?" (pp. 606–612). But Emilia is put off by Frith's "rather Oxfordy manner," an approach to life characterized by his self-dramatizations in convoluted interior dialogues with the appropriated images of others, not by relating to others in actual experience. When Emilia responds to his proposal,

he made odd, sharp gestures, like a drunken man, and he spoke like a drunken man, his eyes turned inward, talking to himself. The woman was no more than a ghost moving inside his own consciousness, and he was addressing her there. [p. 614]

Though he insists, "Now I do *actually* want you, now I actually see you," Lawrence contradicts him: "He never looked at her. His eyes were still turned in" (p. 614).

A corollary of Frith's surface sophistication is his sexual ambiguity. As a result of his Oedipal fixation, his need to "fall on some woman's bosom," he is emotionally impotent: His divorced first wife, Clarissa, observes that he cannot "stand alone for ten minutes" (p. 605); and he himself wonders, when Emilia accepts him, "My God, however am I going to sleep with that woman!" Lawrence provides the sarcastic answer: "His will was ready, . . . and he would manage it somehow." Frith both fears and desires Emilia primarily because she is married to someone else: "the presence of that other man about her" goes "to his head like neat spirits." "Which of the two would fall before him with a greater fall—the woman or the man, her husband?" he wonders (pp. 624–629). As Widmer points out, when Frith takes Emilia, he really "marries the consubstantial husband, the vicarious virility. By taking advantage of the desperate strife that lies between man and woman he has approached reality as close as he can—the erotic perversity of secondhand experience."[11]

The contrast between the two men is established as Pinnegar enters "rather like a blast of wind" and Frith gets up "with a bit of an Oxford wriggle" (p. 616). Pinnegar smells appropriately of "the strange, stale underground," a conventional symbol, as Lawrence observes in the essay on Poe, for the unconscious. As many of Lawrence's heroes get around to doing eventually, Pinnegar strips to the waist in the Laurentian image of dominant masculinity. Like many of these heroes —among them, Cyril in *The White Peacock*, Aaron in *Aaron's Rod*, and the risen man in *The Man Who Died*—Pinnegar is ritualistically bathed by another:

His wife brought a bowl, and with a soapy flannel silently washed his back, right down to the loins, where the trousers were rolled back. The man was entirely oblivious of the stranger—this washing was part of the collier's ritual and nobody existed for the moment. [p. 617]

The function of this ritual as a sacrament of renewal into the vital life of the blood is underlined as Pinnegar gazes "abstractedly, blankly into the fire" until the "colour flushed in his cheeks." Like most Laurentian heroes, from Cyril to Mellors, Pinnegar is an idealized self-portrait: "a man of about thirty-five, in his prime, with a pure smooth skin and no fat on his body. His muscles were not large, but quick, alive with energy." His qualities of moral perception, moreover, parallel his physical qualities. Of the *Commentator*, Frith's periodical, he says, "Seems to me to go a long way round to get nowhere" (pp. 617–619). Declaring that he "won't be made use of," Pinnegar wants "a wife who'll please me, who'll want to please me" (pp. 620–621). Kingsley Widmer stresses, more than Lawrence does, the underlying theme of industrial exploitation: "The embittered miner hates being made into an industrial object, a thing to be used, in the pit. This simple but pervasive point centers Lawrence's fundamental critique of industrial society." But Widmer also observes the larger implications of the theme: "The quality of manhood remains a final purpose and justification and its negation comes from accepting the status of an object, a thing 'to be made use of,' which limits the fullness of being that gives the only meaning to existence."[12]

"THE LAST LAUGH"

In "The Last Laugh" the two antithetical forces clash again, with the resulting execution of the figure of light by the figure of darkness. In the slight plot, Miss James (Dorothy Brett), whose deafness necessitates her carrying "a Marconi listening machine," and Marchbanks (Murry), a "sort of faun on the Cross, with all the malice of the complication," bid goodnight to the thin, red-bearded Lorenzo (Lawrence) (pp. 630–631) and proceed homeward through a veritable barrage of occult phenomena caused by a mysterious supernatural being, the returned god Pan, identified with Lorenzo, who drops from the story after the opening scene. Marchbanks hears the laughter of the elemental being and responds with "wild, neighing, animal laughter" himself. A young policeman approaches, asks about the laughter, and appears doubtful when Marchbanks describes the laughter, which only he hears, as "the most marvelous sound in the world" (p. 633). To Marchbanks's seemingly extrasensory hearing is added Miss James's extrasensory vision. Looking "with brilliant eyes, into the dark holly bushes," she exults, "I always knew I should see him." A Jewish lady in a nearby house, having heard a knock and a call, opens her door, hoping "that something wonderful is going to happen," and asks Marchbanks whether he has knocked. They decide that he must have knocked "without knowing," and he disappears into the house with her (pp. 634–636). As Miss James walks on with the policeman she has the surrealistic sense that occult phenomena are occurring just out of range of sensory perception:

And the whirling snowy air seemed full of presences, full of strange unheard voices. She was used to the sensation of noises taking place where she could not hear. This sensation became very strong. She felt something was happening in the wild air. [p. 638]

Miss James sees "the dark, laughing face" again in a flash of lightning. In contrast, the "tame-animal look" in the policeman's frightened eyes amuses her. In the whistling of the storm she hears voices crying, "He is here! He's come back!" A church window is broken and the church desecrated by this elemental nature-being: "Then a white thing, soaring like a crazy bird, rose up on the wind as if it had wings, and lodged on a black tree outside, struggling." They recognize it as the altar cloth. The wind turns the organ pipes into pan-pipes (pp. 638–640). When the two arrive at Miss James's house, the policeman comes in, cold with fear, to warm himself.

The next morning Miss James's total perspective is changed. She muses on the absurdity of her own paintings, "especially her self-portrait, with its nice brown hair and its slightly opened rabbit-mouth and its baffled, uncertain rabbit-eyes." The housekeeper makes the startling announcement that the policeman, still downstairs, is lame. Looking out of her window, Miss James notes: "Suddenly the world had become quite different: as if some skin or integument had broken, as if the old, mouldering London sky had crackled and rolled back,

like an old skin, shrivelled, leaving an absolutely new blue heaven."
With her new Pan-perspective she also sees the absurdity of her
friendship with Marchbanks, of Marchbanks's chasing the Jewish
woman, of the policeman's "messy," "doggy" devotion, of the state, in
general, of "this being-in-love business." She attributes these changes
in herself to the "extraordinary" being of the night before, the "wonderful face" who "certainly will have the last laugh" (pp. 641–643).
When Marchbanks arrives, she discovers her deafness cured: "Don't
shout," she tells him, "I can hear you quite well" (p. 644). She also
finds that she has lost what has passed for her soul:

. . . I never had one really. It was always fobbed off on me. Soul was the
only thing there was between you and me. Thank goodness it's gone. Haven't
you lost yours? The one that seemed to worry you, like a decayed tooth?
[p. 645]

Downstairs the young policeman confirms in tears the fact that he is
lame: "He slowly pulled off his stocking and showed his white left
foot curiously clubbed, like the weird paw of some animal." As they
marvel at the metamorphosis, Marchbanks suddenly gives "a strange,
yelping cry, like a shot animal. . . . And in the rolling agony of his
eyes was the horrible grin of a man who realises he has made a final,
and this time fatal, fool of himself." With the smell of almond blos-
som in the air Marchbanks dies "in a weird, distorted position, like a
man struck by lightning" (pp. 645–646).

Most critical responses come down to the easily substantiated opinion that "The Last Laugh" fails as a realistic short story. In view of
Murry's comment that it is unclear "what, *in the story,* I was supposed
to have done that deserved death at Pan's hands," it is tempting to see
the havoc which Pan wreaks as nothing more than Lawrence's wish-
fulfillment. Neither character nor setting is convincingly developed,
and Lawrence's use of the story for settling personal scores is irrelevant to critical evaluation. Nevertheless, it is to do the story an injustice, it seems to me, to fail to recognize that Lawrence intended
"The Last Laugh," not as a realistic story, but as a comment on
stereotyped modern existence in the tone of comic irony and the mode
of surrealistic fantasy. As the Great God Pan departed at the birth
of Christ, so now he returns to shatter the Christian church, transform
the policeman, exalt the spinster, and execute the sexually frivolous
intellectual—Lawrence's representatives of modern sterility. The liv-

ing world, it is true, is not presented at all; but what Lawrence re-
gards as the dead world is given shape by means of manipulating
stock characters and symbols drawn from the modern white consciousness. The spinsterish painter with her symbolic deafness, her pru-
dishness, her fear of life; the intellectual dilettante with his irreverent
insistence that the snow, the elemental force of nature which becomes
Pan's instrument of necessary destruction, is only whitewash;[13] and
the young policeman with his baffled devotion to established order, all
function, as befitting their status as "things," as little more than counters of the spiritual deadness which Pan returns to destroy or revive.
Though "The Last Laugh" is a very minor effort, it provides a successful, if anti-realistic, narrative statement of one of Lawrence's
major proposals for the regeneration of the modern world, a revival
of the natural mode of religious perception embodied in the figure
of Pan.

Besides their traditional literary elements, all four stories contain
personal elements which are too much in evidence to be ignored.
Lawrence is, indeed, in most of his work, scarcely less autobiographical than Thomas Wolfe, who, in *The Story of a Novel*, comments on
the term "autobiographical novel" as applied to *Look Homeward,
Angel:*

I protested against this term . . . upon the grounds that any serious work
of creation is of necessity autobiographical and that few more autobiographical works than *Gulliver's Travels* have ever been written. I added that Dr.
Johnson had remarked that a man might turn over half the volumes in his
library to make a single book, and that in a similar way, a novelist might
turn over half the characters in his native town to make a single figure for
his novel.[14]

This is not an unreasonable statement. The difficulty, it may be
charged, is that Lawrence, like Wolfe, rather than combining several
people into one fictional figure often exploits the qualities primarily
of one person. Thus, the writer of fiction becomes vulnerable to negative criticism on other than strictly artistic grounds.
    Wolfe admits that "a young writer is likely . . . to confuse the limits
between actuality and reality."[15] A friend with a personal ax to grind,
it seems to me, is apt to do likewise. Thus, Cecil Gray, who comments
several times on the subject, says:

Lawrence was incapable, in his full-length novels at least, of creating living characters—only heroes, all of them ludicrously Narcissist self-portraits
several times life-size, surrounded by miserable, abject little caricatures of
his friends, many times less than life-size, in order to provide foils and contrasts to the dazzling nobility and transcendent greatness of the central figure, himself.[16]

The extent to which the work of a literary artist is indebted to his
personal experience is, of course, an important consideration in biography and the study of literary sources. What matters in criticism,
however, is the effectiveness of the finished work of art. Lawrence's
heroes, despite their origin in the author's narcissism, usually emerge,
Gray to the contrary, as credible characters. The figures of Lawrence's
friends, furthermore, are seldom merely miniature foils for Lawrence's
ego-figure. But in establishing the moral norm against which the deviation is satirically measured, the ego-figure often has the function
of correcting the friend-figure for the reader's instruction. Because
they exaggerate flaws, satirical portraits, if taken literally, may seem
unfair. Even so, Lawrence's portrait of Murry in the four satirical
stories and Murry's self-portrait in his subsequent correspondence
with Frieda do not differ in essentials. In both treatments of his character in 1923–1924, Murry emerges as a somewhat frightened, dependent person, who is concerned more with self-dramatization than with
self-knowledge, more with self-justification than with self-consciousness. It is, rather, Lawrence's ego-figures that are embellished. In actuality Lawrence was neither the descendant of a baron, a distinction
which he borrows from Frieda for the character of Alan Anstruther,
nor himself a common laborer, the status of his father which he borrows for the character of Pinnegar. Such embellished characterizations
of the ego-figures, however, should be viewed, not as personal dis-
guises which fool no one, but as literary personae which function
metaphorically in the stories in which they appear.

In these four stories the figure of Murry, as Matthew, Philip Farquhar, Jimmy Frith, and Marchbanks, characterizes the moral trivial-
ity of the modern waste land of sterile, white consciousness. In three
of the stories the figure of Lawrence himself, as Alan Anstruther,
Pinnegar, and Lorenzo, who is symbolically identified with Pan, defines not only the moral norm by which the deviation of the Murry-
figure is measured but also the means by which the waste land might
be regenerated, the ancient, dark, blood consciousness.

NOTES

1. Harry T. Moore, *Poste Restante: A Lawrence Travel Calendar* (Berkeley and Los Angeles: University of California Press, 1956), pp. 69–72.

2. (New York: The Viking Press, 1934), p. 141.

3. Knud Merrild, *A Poet and Two Painters: A Memoir of D. H. Lawrence* (New York: The Viking Press, 1939), p. 340.

4. Quoted in F. A. Lea, *The Life of John Middleton Murry* (London: Methuen and Co. Ltd., 1959), p. 118.

5. *Frieda Lawrence: The Memoirs and Correspondence,* ed. E. W. Tedlock, Jr. (New York: Alfred A. Knopf, 1964). The correspondence between Frieda Lawrence and John Middleton Murry, cited in my text by date, is quoted from pp. 279–368.

6. This account of the Café Royal dinner is taken from Catherine Carswell, *The Savage Pilgrimage: A Narrative of D. H. Lawrence* (London: Chatto and Windus, 1932), pp. 207–213; and John Middleton Murry, *Reminiscences of D. H. Lawrence* (New York: Henry Holt and Co., 1933), pp. 168–170.

7. "The Three Women in a Man's Life," in *Art and Psychoanalysis,* ed. William Phillips (New York: Criterion Books, 1957), p. 163.

8. *The White Goddess: A Historical Grammar of Poetic Myth,* amended and enlarged ed. (New York: Vintage Books, 1958), p. 61.

9. Kingsley Widmer, *The Art of Perversity: D. H. Lawrence's Shorter Fictions* (Seattle: University of Washington Press, 1962), pp. 53–54.

10. *D. H. Lawrence,* 2d ed. (London: Arthur Barker Ltd., 1966), p. 99.

11. Widmer, p. 144.

12. Ibid., p. 143.

13. For an elaboration of this point, see Harry T. Moore, *D. H. Lawrence: His Life and Works,* rev. ed. (New York: Twayne Publishers, Inc., 1964), pp. 216–218.

14. In *Only the Dead Know Brooklyn* (New York: The New American Library, Signet Books, 1952), p. 117.

15. Ibid., p. 118.

16. In Edward Nehls, ed., *D. H. Lawrence: A Composite Biography* (Madison: University of Wisconsin Press, 1957), I, 436.

CHAPTER FIVE

The Quest for Symbol and Myth

LAWRENCE'S TASK in the American period was to find symbols adequate to express the waste land of contemporary life and a myth potent enough to transform it. The four anti-Murry stories, though they are more serious works than most critics have allowed, are quite minor efforts. Furthermore, though Lawrence successfully embodies in the Murry-figures his vision of the emotional sterility of the white consciousness, his choice of Murry as a counter in this allegorical statement was dictated, undeniably, more by personal than by universal considerations. Thus, whatever the quality of the stories, Lawrence leaves himself open to the charge of forsaking artistic distance for personal invective, of emotion, not remembered in tranquility, but unleashed in the heat of battle. In three short works of the period, the tales *The Princess* and *The Woman Who Rode Away* and the short novel *St. Mawr*, though he follows his usual practice of turning his friends into story material, Lawrence finds in symbol and myth the means to a more universal statement.

THE PRINCESS

In *The Princess*, as John B. Vickery has suggested, myth "operates as a kind of second story, almost a double plot which illuminates the basic story by suggesting a link with man's earliest forms of belief and behavior." The basic story, concomitantly, functions on one level "as a mythic reenactment, as a method of telling a past story through what is now being done."[1] As structural and thematic motifs, Lawrence employs, first, as in *Lady Chatterley's Lover* (1928), the fairy tale of the Sleeping Beauty, and, second, as in *The Plumed Serpent*, the "separation—initiation—return" pattern of romance, which Joseph Campbell, using Joyce's term, calls the monomyth. But Lawrence inverts the pattern of quest as the aging princess rejects her would-be prince only to "return" to an even deeper slumber than before. The result is a brilliantly realized ironic romance.

Mary Henrietta Urquhart, whose mother calls her "My Dollie," a name suggesting, as in Ibsen, possession of the plaything rather than love of the person, and whose father calls her "My Princess," a title with multiple allusions to aristocracy of birth, social snobbishness, and the unreality of romance, strikingly resembles her sleeping proto-types. The Germanic Briar Rose falls into her hundred-year sleep as the result of a curse laid upon her by the fairy who was not invited to the King's feast honoring her birth. The Norse Brynhild, as punish-ment for disobeying Odin, is put to sleep until a man shall awaken her. In both tales the charm is inculcated by a magic circle: Briar Rose's castle is surrounded by a hedge of thorns, and Brynhild's couch is encircled with fire. As Campbell explains, "This is an image of the magic circle drawn about the personality by the dragon power of the fixating parent," resulting in "an impotence to put off the infantile ego, with its sphere of emotional relationships and ideals." With the parents guarding the threshold, one "fails to make the passage through the door and come to birth in the world without."[2]

Dollie Urquhart's world is defined by the family circle. Lawrence subtly mythicizes her father, Colin, the mad descendant of Scottish kings: "He looked like some old Celtic hero. He looked as if he should have worn a greyish kilt and a sporran, and shown his knees. His voice came direct out of the hushed Ossianic past" (p. 473). Her mother Lawrence disposes of quickly with the omission of particulars that is characteristic of fairy tales. Having "lived three years in the mist and glamour of her husband's presence," "she had no great desire to live. So when the baby was two years old she suddenly died" (pp. 473–474). Dollie herself is characterized by juxtaposed contradictions: "To her father, she was The Princess. To her Boston aunts and uncles she was just *Dollie Urquhart, poor little thing*." Hostesses comment, "She is so quaint and old-fashioned; such a lady, poor little mite!" And the author explains, "She was always grown up; she never really grew up. Always strangely wise, and always childish" (pp. 473–476).

As Dollie develops, or rather fails to develop, under Colin's tutelage, she becomes fixated, as in the extended sleep of her prototypes, at an Oedipal level, suspended in a storybook world in which children pretend to be adults, adults behave like children, and the way to maturity is effectively obstructed for all. Colin early puts Dollie in the ambivalent position of masking fearful distrust with polite condescension. His method of doing so is revealed in his baroque fable of peeling the onion:

"You peel everything away from people, and there is a green, upright demon in every man and woman; and this demon is a man's real self, and a woman's real self. It doesn't really care about anybody, it belongs to the demons and the primitive fairies, who never care." [p. 475]

Dollie, Colin says, is the last of the "royal fairy women," but she must keep this fact a secret since others, envious of her state, will try to kill her. She must, therefore, treat others with "Noblesse oblige" but not, since they are commoners, as her equals (pp. 475–476). Colin is presenting, of course, a version of the "pristine unconscious," which Lawrence defines in *Psychoanalysis and the Unconscious* as "that essential unique nature of every individual creature, which is, by its very nature, unanalysable, undefinable, inconceivable" (p. 15). But when Colin uses the fable only to impose on Dollie his fantasy of aristocratic birth into the privileged class, a far cry from the Laurentian aristocracy of blood consciousness, his perversion of the concept becomes clear. The psychological phenomenon of the *folie à deux*, "the occurrence in two close associates of the same mental disorder at the same time,"[3] may prove instructive. Theodore Lidz and his associates, on the basis of their study of schizophrenic patients and their families, concluded that parents often transmit their irrational or delusional conceptions directly to their children without elaboration; thus, Lidz enlarges the concept to *folie à famille*.[4] The effect of the Urquharts' *folie à famille* is Dollie's education in basic distrust: "The Princess learned her lesson early—the first lesson, of absolute reticence, the impossibility of intimacy with any other than her father; the second lesson, of naive, slightly benevolent politeness." Illustrations of these generalizations are profuse. In refusing an invitation to live with her grandfather, for example, Dollie says: "You are so very kind. But Papa and I are such an old couple, you see, such a crochety old couple, living in a world of our own."

In this world Dollie's potential womanhood sleeps: "She was so exquisite and such a little virgin." Mediterranean cabmen and porters, standing in for Lawrence, sense in her a "sterile impertinence towards the things *they* felt most"—"*beauté male*" and "the phallic mystery" —and long to crush the "barren flower" of her maidenhood. Dollie senses their hatred, but, Lawrence puns, "she did not lose her head. She quietly paid out money and turned away" (pp. 476–477). As Sigmund Freud observes, such girls, "to the delight of their parents, retain their full infantile love far beyond puberty. . . ." Even as wives they remain "sexually anesthetic." To Freud, "this shows that the apparently nonsexual love for parents and sexual love are nourished from the same source, i.e., that the first merely corresponds to an infantile fixation of the libido."[5] In the sleeplike fixity of her personality, Dollie "had that quality of the sexless fairies, she did not change." In contrast to Lawrence's sexual sleepers who are awakened by some phallic representative of the sun god, Dollie is languid, "like a flower that has blossomed in a shadowy place." When she is thirty-eight, her father dies: "She was the Princess, and sardonically she looked out on a princeless world" (p. 479).

Though Dollie retains "the idea of marriage," she now transfers what Lawrence calls her "passion for her mad father" to Colin's nurse-companion, Miss Charlotte Cummins. When the two women move west to a New Mexican dude ranch, the Rancho del Cerro Gordo, the Sleeping Princess encounters her dispossessed and fragmented Prince, Domingo Romero, the son of an old San Christobal family of Spanish landowners who, as the result of their own inertia and the invasion of the white man, have become mere Mexican peasants. The heir apparent to this ruin works as a guide on the ranch, where the emotionally lifeless tourists "rarely *see* anything, inwardly," of the "spark" in the middle of his eyes. Dollie does see it, however, and promptly concludes that Romero is a "gentleman" with a "fine demon" (pp. 482–483). Not surprisingly, Dollie conceives a desire for Romero to fulfill, in relation to her, both his literal and symbolic functions as guide: "She wanted to look over the mountains into their secret heart" (p. 487). In a fictional rendering of Lawrence's biographical experience Dollie, Miss Cummins, and Romero set out on a three days' journey to the top of the mountain ridge. The Honorable Dorothy Brett has recorded a day's ride she made with Lawrence and Mrs. Rachel Hawk to the top of the ridge above San Christobal canyon.[6] Dollie Urquhart, in several significant ways, resembles Brett; and Romero, even in his fragmentation, embodies some of Lawrence's key ideas. Yet in *The Princess* Lawrence maintains the aesthetic distance necessary to unity of plot, character, and setting in universal rather than merely personal or local significance.

From this point to the end of the story the structural and thematic principle is an ironically inverted rendering of the monomyth. Romero, dressed in Laurentian black and riding a black horse, is the mythic guide, whose function, like that of supernatural helpers as various as the Virgil of Dante's *Inferno* and the Mephistopheles of Goethe's *Faust,* is to lure "the innocent soul into realms of trial." As the "supernatural principle of guardianship and direction," this figure unites in himself "all the ambiguities of the unconscious," thus demonstrating both the unconscious source of support for the conscious personality and the "inscrutability of the guide that we are following. . . ."[7] Romero as guide has chthonic qualities associated with his negative task of peeling the onion of Dollie's social self. When Miss Cummins turns back, the last support for Dollie's dependent state vanishes. Reaching the ridge with Romero, Dollie gazes down into the primordial core of the Rocky Mountains: "It frightened the Princess, it was *so* inhuman" (p. 496). What frightens Dollie is the vision of independent, amoral, even impersonal selfhood, the cosmic identity of what Lawrence calls in *Fantasia of the Unconscious* "the first and supreme knowledge that *I am I*" (p. 75). For the "intestinal knot" of the mountains into which she stares is the ultimate green demon of the earth, the solar plexus of the cosmos, the navel of the world. As Campbell explains, the quest of the hero of the monomyth is "the unlocking and release again of the flow of life into the body of the world." The hidden source of this torrent is under the World Navel, "the center of the symbolic circle of the universe": "Beneath this spot is the earth-supporting head of the cosmic serpent, the dragon, symbolical of the waters of the abyss, which are the divine life-creative energy and substance of the demiurge, the world-generative aspect of immortal being."[8]

As Dollie and Romero descend, they move, as if in answer to the mythic summons, out of society and across the threshold into the center of experience. According to Campbell, "the call rings up the curtain, always, on a mystery of transfiguration—a rite, or moment, of spiritual passage, which, when complete, amounts to a dying and a birth."[9] Since such a transfiguring experience is hardly subject to deliberate, conscious control, both Dollie's and Romero's minds are appropriately numb. When they reach the cabin, they find this artifact of civilization all but taken over by nature: "The roof had gone—but Romero had laid on thick spruce boughs" (p. 500). That night, however, instead of being transfigured, Dollie feels trapped: "She dreamed it was snowing, and the snow was falling on her through the roof, . . . and she was going to be buried alive" (p. 503). Lawrence's comment in *Studies in Classic American Literature* on Poe's premature burial stories, which the dream parallels, is critically appropriate to Dollie's character: "All this underground vault business . . . symbolizes that which takes place *beneath* the consciousness. On top all is fair-spoken. Beneath there is awful murderous extremity of burying alive" (p. 79). Dollie's ambivalence about Romero reveals the symbolic value of the dream: "She wanted warmth, protection, she wanted to be taken away from herself. And at the same time, . . . she wanted to keep herself intact, intact, untouched, that no one should have any power over her . . ." (p. 503). When Dollie complains that she is cold, Romero offers to warm her. Contrasting the extremes of heat and cold, they also represent the opposite values of body and mind, blood and nerve, the sensual and the spiritual, the organic and the inorganic. As Lawrence explains in the essay on Poe: "In sensual love, it is the two blood-systems . . . which sweep up into pure contact. . . . In spiritual love, the contact is purely nervous" (pp. 66–67). When Romero comes into Dollie's bed "with a terrible animal warmth that seemed to annihilate her," he pants "like an animal." For Dollie, however, the sexual act is purely mental: "She had never, never wanted to be given over to this. But she had *willed* that it should happen to her" (p. 504). In *Psychoanalysis and the Unconscious* Lawrence defines idealism as "the motivizing of the great affective sources by means of ideas mentally derived" (p. 11): "I may have ideals if I like," he adds in *Fantasia of the Unconscious,* "but I have no right to ask another to have these ideals. And to impose *any* ideals upon a child as it grows is almost criminal. . . . It results in neurasthenia" (p. 90). Dollie's father had imposed upon her his own delusional "ideals" of aristocracy. The imbalance thus set up between the opposites of her personality makes impossible any but a willed, mental relationship with Romero, and so leads to his psychic ruin, too. In the face of her obstinate coldness he alternates ambivalently between wheedling: "You sure won't act mean to me," and despair: "I sure don't mind hell fire. . . . After this" (pp. 506–508).

Dollie, having irrevocably rejected the mythic call to adventure and transfiguration, dissolves in helpless hysterics. According to Campbell, rejection of the summons, essentially, is a refusal to surrender old modes of being for new ones. The future, thus, "is regarded not in terms of an unremitting series of deaths and births, but as though one's present system of ideals, virtues, goals, and advantages were to be fixed and made secure." The refusal, however, results, not in conservation, but in negation. The hero's "flowering world becomes a wasteland of dry stones and his life feels meaningless. . . .

All he can do is create new problems for himself and await the gradual approach of his disintegration."[10] The principle is illustrated brilliantly in the conclusion of *The Princess*. Dollie, freed from the cabin by forest rangers, who kill Romero in an exchange of gunfire, remains the prisoner of her own psychic virginity, her sexual sleep. Years later, still fixated in her daughter state of dependency, Dollie infuses her experience at the World Navel with delusion: "Since my accident in the mountains, when a man went mad and shot my horse from under me, and my guide had to shoot him dead, I have never felt quite myself." Symbolically, through her marriage to a much older man, Dollie even gets her father back (p. 512).

THE WOMAN WHO RODE AWAY

Written in the summer of 1924, between the two halves of *The Plumed Serpent*, Lawrence's tale *The Woman Who Rode Away* has affinities with the novel. The problems presented by any attempt at evaluation, however, are attested to by the opposites of adverse and favorable criticism with which it has met. The extremes are stated by Anthony West and Graham Hough. To West the story seems a "forgery": expecting to find a "living religion" in Mexican Indian culture, Lawrence found, in West's opinion, "the dead carcass of a religion . . . existing only as a formal gesture for the benefit of the American tourists":

Lawrence, believing in the life of the body as the supreme human fulfilment, was being entirely untrue to his belief in making his white woman find the way to fulfilment by accepting death at the hands of the Indians. The effect is as dead as the religious work of the smart rationalist painters of the eighteenth century who tried to counterfeit mysticism with the contortions of eroticism.[11]

To Hough, on the other hand, the story seems "successful": "a mode midway between realism and symbolism" that permits transformation of "the actual, the given without any breach of unity." The question of whether Lawrence counterfeited the religious motif is irrelevant: "We are not discussing the actualities of Mexican religion: we are discussing Lawrence's religion projected into the Mexican scene." The woman's sacrifice by the practitioners of the death cult is admirably, if horribly, realized. As Hough puts it, "I should say for myself that *The Woman Who Rode Away* is his completest artistic achievement. It is also his profoundest comment on the world of his time."[12]

A more partisan, but nonetheless accurate, observation on the technique and achievement of *The Woman Who Rode Away* is F. R. Leavis's statement on the ritualistic manner of the narrative:

By a marvellous triumph of incantation—incantation that proceeds by a compellingly vivid and matter-of-fact particularity—it succeeds supremely in something that *The Plumed Serpent* fails in. It imagines the old pagan Mexican religion as something real and living; living enough for its devotees to entertain the confident hope of reconquering Mexico.[13]

Most unfavorable comments on *The Woman Who Rode Away* come from critics who, like West, take the story literally. Calling the story a fable has, I think, the advantage of recognizing Lawrence's emphasis on the ritualistic rather than the realistic aspects of the story. Perhaps the critical confusion about *The Woman Who Rode Away* can be resolved by examining the myths, rituals, and ideas that Lawrence fuses into a single religious metaphor.

First, there is in the story more than a touch of the monomyth. The summons to adventure comes in a chance conversation with guests who are discussing an Indian tribe living deep in the mountains of Chihuahua and following, as one says, "howling and heathen practices, more or less indecent," or, as the other puts it, "old, old religions and mysteries": "And this particular vague enthusiasm for unknown Indians found a full echo in the woman's heart. . . . She felt it was her destiny to wander into the secret haunts of these timeless, mysterious, marvellous Indians of the mountains." Lawrence's word about the "monotony of her life" and her longing to be "free" (pp. 549–550) makes clear that the call is to spiritual passage from constriction to freedom.[14] The destination of her journey, the World Navel, as well as its association with her own solar plexus, becomes apparent on her first night away from home:

She was not sure that she had not heard, during the night, a great crash at the centre of herself, which was the crash of her own death. Or else it was a crash at the centre of the earth, and meant something big and mysterious. [p. 552]

The woman makes a journey of three days, in both linear and mythic time, on a road of trials. The young Indian who speaks Spanish and who, from his trips to Mexico City and Chicago, has gained some knowledge of the white world, is, appropriately, the woman's guide on her perilous journey from the white man's culture to his. He repeatedly poses the choice between alternative modes of being, and in his simultaneously threatening and solicitous manner, he unites the ambiguities of her own unconscious.[15] Another Indian, with a malevolence without purpose except to destroy her will, repeatedly strikes her horse with a stick so that the woman is jerked forward in the saddle painfully (pp. 555–556). To fulfill her desire of entering the Indian village the woman, at the expense of dignity and comfort, must laboriously cross the dangerous razor's edge of the mountain ridge (p. 558). Julian Moynahan, who takes such scenes at realistic value, finds this "one of the most depressing images in all Lawrence: a blonde woman crawling on hands and knees along a narrow mountain ledge, while her two Indian captors walk easily erect, . . . both indifferent to her discomfort and danger."[16] But the ritualistic value of the image should be familiar, if not from the Katha Upanishad 3:14:

> A sharpened edge of a razor, hard to traverse,
> A difficult path is this,

then certainly from Chrétien de Troyes' account of Lancelot's crossing the sword-bridge to rescue Guinevere from the Castle of Death. As the woman's temptation to hurl herself down suggests, the narrow ledge bridges the abyss of damnation. As in the Persian test of the sword-bridge at the Last Judgment, "the sinful will fall into the abyss, but for the pious the edge broadens out into a smooth and pleasant way, leading to Paradise."[17] Thus, the Indians, who preserve the Laurentian piety of dark consciousness, walk erect, and only the woman, guilty of the sin of whiteness, is in peril. As Joseph Campbell explains, the road of trials "is the process of dissolving, transcending, or transmuting the infantile images of our personal past."[18]

The woman, however, still has much to undergo. In Campbell's words, "The original departure into the land of trials represented only the beginning of the long and really perilous path of initiatory conquests and moments of illumination."[19] Taken before the *cacique*, the woman begins her metamorphosis from white lady to sacrificial victim. The Indians, despite her protests, remove her clothes, and the "old man moistened his finger-tips at his mouth, and most delicately touched her on the breasts and on the body, then on the back. And she winced strangely each time . . . as if Death itself were touching her." Then she is given new clothing suggesting her new identity: "a long white cotton shift, that came to her knees: then a tunic of thick blue woollen stuff, embroidered with scarlet and green flowers" (p. 564). Subsequently, she learns the symbolic value of her color, blue:

"It is the colour of the wind. It is the colour of what goes away and is never coming back. . . . It is the colour of the dead. And it is the colour that stands away off, looking at us from the distance, that cannot come near to us." [p. 574]

The woman undergoes ritual purgation by means of a liquor brewed from herbs and honey which induces uncontrollable vomiting, the symbolic regurgitation of her old life, and a languorous heightening of the senses so that she can hear "the sound of the evening flowers unfolding" (p. 565). In another trance, she even hears the little dog the Indians have given her "conceive, in her tiny womb, and begin to be complex, with young" (p. 568). The woman also undergoes ritual purification by being bathed and rubbed with oil in "a long, strange, hypnotic massage" (pp. 576–577). According to Campbell,

the ordeal is a deepening of the problem of the first threshold and the question is still in balance: Can the ego put itself to death? . . . Meanwhile, there will be a multitude of preliminary victories, unretainable ecstasies, and momentary glimpses of the wonderful land.[20]

The purpose of the woman's sacrifice, as she learns, has to do with the regeneration of the world. According to the Indians' myth of creation, the sun as male principle and the moon as female principle, in their world-generative cosmic intercourse, parallel the creative function of instinctual sexuality in man:

"So the woman, she asks the moon to come into her cave, inside her. And the man, he draws the sun down till he has the power of the sun. . . . Then when the man gets a woman, the sun goes into the cave of the moon, and that is how everything in the world starts." [p. 571]

When the Indians weakened and lost their power with sun and moon, the whites stole them. " 'White men don't know what they are doing with the sun, and white women don't know what they do with the moon' " (p. 571). The idea is central to Lawrence's thinking, for blood consciousness is, finally, cosmic knowledge. He elaborates the point subsequently in *Apocalypse:*

In the centuries before Ezekial and John, the sun was still a magnificent reality, men drew forth from him strength and splendour, and gave him back homage and lustre and thanks. But in us, the connection is broken, the responsive centres are dead. Our sun is a quite different thing from the cosmic sun of the ancients, so much more trivial. . . . We have lost the cosmos, by coming out of responsive connection with it, and this is our chief tragedy. [pp. 41–42]

The loss is the more tragic in that creative energy, perverted, becomes destructive:

The sun is a great source of blood-vitality, it streams strength to us. But once we resist the sun, and say: It is a mere ball of gas!—then the very streaming vitality of sunshine turns into subtle disintegrative force in us, and undoes us. The same with the moon, the planets, the great stars. They are either our makers or our unmakers. There is no escape. [p. 45]

But there is redemption. The informing idea of *The Woman Who Rode Away* is the Indians' myth of rebirth: "When a white woman sacrifice herself to our gods, then our gods will begin to make the world again, and the white man's gods will fall to pieces" (p. 570)

On the shortest day of the year the myth is fulfilled as the woman attended by "lurid, dancing priests," is taken to a mountain cave where, stripped of her garments, she is placed on a flat stone for the ritual in which she has acquiesced. In keeping with the solar creation myth, Lawrence places her sacrifice at the very moment when the setting sun shines through the shaft of ice at the cave's mouth. Once again, with the ritual killing of the white *pharmakos,* the sun enters the cave of the moon in cosmic intercourse. From this navel center the world-generative waters will flow (pp. 578–579).

If the fable of *The Woman Who Rode Away* is patterned on the monomyth, the theme derives from the rite of human sacrifice, itself a construct of the monomyth. The religious ritual of the Dying and Reviving God, the world over, re-enacts the natural ritual of the annual death and rebirth of the sun. Robert Graves recounts the semi-annual sacrifice of the twin Hercules-figures of European solar festivals. The first Hercules, sacrificed at midsummer after a half-year reign, is made drunk with mead, led into a circle of twelve stones and brutally killed. The whole tribe, to insure its vigor and fruitfulness, is sprinkled with his blood. His tanist, the second Hercules, then reigns until midwinter, when he too is sacrificed by the new Hercules.[21] William Tyler Olcott relates a Scandinavian tradition of making bonfires of pine boughs at the summer solstice on the death of the sun god Balder to light his way to the nether world and of burning a yule log and lighting fir trees at the winter solstice on his rebirth to light his way to the heavens.[22] Alan W. Watts, in discussing the infusion of Christian ritual with solar mythology, points out that "because the sun itself in both its daily and annual course is seen as a type of Christ, the Sun of Justice," the Christian year, beginning with Advent, "is rather significantly integrated with the cycle of the sun." The feast of the Nativity coincides approximately with the winter solstice, sometimes known as "the Birth of the Sun," a time when "the sun is at its lowest meridian and is about to begin once more its upward journey to the midheaven."[23] Such solar myths and rituals as these are the basis of Aztec rituals of human sacrifice. Sir James George Frazer reports that an effigy of the god Huitzilopochtli, "fashioned out of seeds of various sorts, which were kneaded into a dough with the blood of children," was sacrificed and eaten by the Aztecs in the festival of the winter solstice in December.[24] And Victor W. von Hagen says that "the adoration of the eating of the corn, an eight-day feast" at midsummer in the eighth month (2–21 July) of the eighteen months of the Aztec calendar, "could not get under way until the priests had dispatched a slave girl, beautifully attired to impersonate the Goddess of Young Corn."[25] Clearly, the rite of human sacrifice is in part a fertility ritual deriving from solar festivals celebrating the death and rebirth of the sun.

According to Alfonso Caso, director of archaeology in the National Museum of Mexico and director of the National Institute of Anthropology and History in Mexico, "the essence of human sacrifice among the Aztecs lay in the conception of the interdependence of man and his gods." The Aztecs considered the victim a messenger who was to bear their supplication to the gods. For this reason, they treated sacrificial victims solicitously, sometimes even revering them as gods.[26] As Laurette Séjourné explains this interdependence between the divine and the human, since the deity "detaches a little from itself in every creature," it would totally deplete itself were the individual to destroy his particle "instead of returning it still brighter than before": "That is, creation is held to be impossible except through sacrifice: the sacrifice of the Sun dismembered among human kind; . . . the sacrifice of men to restore the sun's original unity."[27] The concept underlay even the form of the sacrifice. As Caso describes the rite, the priests placed the victim "on a stone called *téchcatl*, similar in shape to a sugar loaf or cone with the top somewhat flattened out." Four priests pinioned his arms and legs and laid him on his back on the *téchcatl* with his chest arched upwards. "Then a fifth priest took the flint knife and plunged it into the breast, tore out the heart, and

offered it to the gods."[28] The concept of human sacrifice to replenish
the source of life was familiar to Lawrence in the rituals of tree worship among the ancient Germanic tribes of Europe. As he notes in
Movements in European History: "The tree-worship, the worship of
the Tree of Life seems always to have entailed human sacrifice. Life
is the fruit of that Tree. But the Tree is dark and terrible, it demands
life back again" (p. 59).

Another practice of the ancient religion which has survived among
the Chilchui Indians in *The Woman Who Rode Away* is the use of
hallucinogenic drugs to heighten sensory perception and psychic experience. Interestingly, Mme. Séjourné gives an account of a tribe
called the Huicholes, still living in northwestern Mexico, who have
preserved many ancient Nahuatl beliefs and rituals.[29] According to
Frazer, this tribe treats "as a demi-god a species of cactus which
throws the eater into a state of ecstasy."[30] The Huichol Indians apparently are the basis for Lawrence's Chilchui tribe, whose name is
almost an anagram of theirs. Irene Nicholson, critic and translator of
Nahuatl poetry, says that the poets sometimes used mushrooms to
induce visions.[31] And Aldous Huxley, who in *Brave New World* presents Lawrence's primitivism in the figure of a New Mexican Indian,
says of peyote in *Brave New World Revisited:*

It permits the Indians who use it in their religious rites to enter paradise,
and to feel at one with the beloved community, without making them pay
for the privilege by anything worse than the ordeal of having to chew on
something with a revolting flavor and of feeling somewhat nauseated for an
hour or two.[32]

Although the religion of *The Woman Who Rode Away* may be,
as Hough suggests, projected out of Lawrence's own consciousness
into the Mexican scene, it is beautifully integrated with rituals and
values of the Nahuatl religion, which was already there. If the sacrifice of the woman is to be efficacious, she must be identified, first, with
traditional sacrificial victims of solar rituals and, second, with the
white world, which is being sacrificed symbolically through her. Lawrence relates the woman to the traditional *pharmakos* of fertility rites
by associating her with vegetation: with the pine boughs of her shelter
and bed on the journey, with the ears of corn in the maize fields she
passes on entering the village, with the red flowers in the garden outside her cell, and with the scarlet and green flowers embroidered on
her tunic. As in the solar rituals of the Aztecs and other primitive

peoples, the time of human sacrifice among Lawrence's Chilchui Indians is the winter solstice. The Indian's loss of power and the white man's theft of the sun are related, by implication, to the sun's journey into the underworld. Thus, the function of the woman's blood sacrifice is the rebirth of the sun and the salvation of the world.

Since the woman's sacrifice symbolizes the ritual death of the white man's gods, and thus of their spiritual potential in the world, the woman must both represent those gods and, in keeping with the Indians' myth of rebirth, demonstrably reject them for the Indians' gods. Lawrence presents the woman as a representative of western culture in decline by keeping her nameless but giving her a husband who, like Sir Clifford Chatterley, owns mines which encroach upon nature. Hating anything physical, this mine owner, Lawrence says in a telling phrase, "admired his wife to extinction" (p. 547). Lawrence also presents the woman as a representative of the white man's religion. She is identified with Christ as sacrificial victim in a number of significant parallels: her age, thirty-three; her journey of three days, a metaphorical descent into hell; her ritualistic anointing with oil and perfume; her sign of peace to the ancient *cacique,* a symbolic Gethsemane; her cup of liquor, an analogy to the chalice of the Last Supper; her being stripped for the sacrifice; and finally her death for the sins of her race and the redemption of the world. She is also associated with the Blessed Virgin by means of her color, blue, the color of fidelity and of the heavens. The repeated emphasis on her blondeness suggests her symbolic role as queen of heaven.

Lawrence has the woman reject the Christian God four times for the gods of the Indians. When she first meets the three Indians, the young Indian asks her where she is going and what she wants to do. She replies, "I want to visit the Chilchui Indians—to see their houses and to know their gods" (p. 554). On her arrival when the chief asks whether she wants to bring the white man's God to the Chilchui, she replies, "No. . . . I came away from the white man's God myself. I came to look for the God of the Chilchui" (p. 560). When she is brought before the *cacique,* the young Indian translates his question, "Do you bring your heart to the god of the Chilchui?" Acquiescing in her own sacrifice, she replies, "Tell him yes" (p. 563). Finally, when the young Indian explains that his people are trying to recover their lost power with the sun, she says, "I hope you will get him back" (pp. 572–573).

By offering herself as living sacrifice, the woman goes beyond personality and achieves cosmic identity:

More and more her ordinary personal consciousness had left her, she had gone into that other state of passional cosmic consciousness, like one who is drugged. The Indians, with their heavily religious natures, had made her succumb to their vision. [p. 574]

Her consciousness is "passional" in the dual sense of suffering and sexuality, with reference, in both senses, to the cosmos. Her heightening awareness of her religious role parallels the sensations of her drugged state. Critics who object to her being literally drugged forget that in this state she loses will and gains direct, experiential knowledge of her own participation in the cosmos.

In the figure of the *cacique* with his face "like dark glass" (p. 563) Lawrence unites the ambiguities of his theme. The Christian reference of this dual allusion is, of course, to Saint Paul: "For now we see through a glass, darkly; but then face to face: now I know in part; but then I shall know even as also I am known" (1 Corinthians 13:12) The Aztec reference is to Tezcatlipoca, Lord of the Smoking Mirror whose sacrifice fell at about the time of the Christian Easter. On this day a youth, in the role of Tezcatlipoca for which he had been preparing for a year, was sacrificed. Although the sacrifice was a spring ritual, Mme. Séjourné suggests that the ceremonies of the twenty days preceding the event symbolize the winter solstice:

If the winter solstice reproduces on a larger scale the daily drama of light imprisoned by darkness, the prisoner's death must signify his liberation . . . This hypothesis seems, moreover, to be proved by the fact that the ceremonies immediately following upon the death of Tezcatlipoca (Earth Sun) are dedicated to Huitzilpochtli (Sun of the Centre), who seems to rise from the sacrificed body of the Lord of the Smoking Mirror. . . .[33]

The reiterated image of the *cacique* as a "glassy-dark old man" (p 564), with "black, glass-like, intent eyes" (p. 573), which, at the sacrifice of the woman, are "fixed like black mirrors on the sun" (p 581), identifies him metaphorically as Tezcatlipoca, in whose place the woman, representing the white race that holds the sun captive will be sacrificed. In the final image of the story, the *cacique* waits for the rays of the phallic sun to penetrate the yonic cave in an illustration of the Indians' myth of creation. What the woman sees "through a glass, darkly," then, is not merely the fact of her sacrifice but also its meaning: the rebirth of the sun and the flow of creativity in the body of the cosmos.

NOTES

1. "Myth and Ritual in the Shorter Fiction of D. H. Lawrence," *Modern Fiction Studies*, V (Spring, 1959), 70.

2. Joseph Campbell, *The Hero with a Thousand Faces*, The Bollingen Series XVII (New York: Pantheon Books, Inc., 1949), p. 62.

3. Horace B. English and Ava Champney English, *A Comprehensive Dictionary of Psychological and Psychoanalytical Terms* (New York, London, and Toronto: Longmans, Green and Co., 1958), p. 212.

4. Silvano Arieti, "Schizophrenia: The Manifest Symptomatology, the Psychodynamic and Formal Mechanisms," *American Handbook of Psychiatry* (New York: Basic Books, Inc., 1959), I, 469–470.

5. *Three Essays on the Theory of Sexuality*, in *The Complete Psychological Works of Sigmund Freud*, Vol. VII, trans. and ed. James Strachey in collaboration with Anna Freud (London: The Hogarth Press and The Institute of Psycho-Analysis, 1953), p. 227.

6. *Lawrence and Brett: A Friendship* (Philadelphia: J. B. Lippincott Co., 1933), pp. 149–152.

7. Campbell, *The Hero with a Thousand Faces*, pp. 72–73.

8. Ibid., pp. 40–41.

9. Ibid., p. 51.

10. Ibid., pp. 59–60.

11. *D. H. Lawrence*, 2d ed. (London: Arthur Barker Ltd., 1966), pp. 96–97.

12. *The Dark Sun: A Study of D. H. Lawrence* (New York: The Macmillan Co., 1957), pp. 140–146.

13. *D. H. Lawrence: Novelist* (New York: Alfred A. Knopf, 1956), pp. 342–343.

14. See Campbell, *The Hero with a Thousand Faces*, p. 51.

15. Ibid., pp. 72–73.

16. *The Deed of Life: The Novels and Tales of D. H. Lawrence* (Princeton: Princeton University Press, 1963), p. 178.

17. These examples are cited in Heinrich Zimmer, *The King and the Corpse: Tales of the Soul's Conquest of Evil*, ed. Joseph Campbell, The Bollingen Series XI (New York: Pantheon Books, Inc., 1948), pp. 171–172.

18. *The Hero with a Thousand Faces*, p. 101.

19. Ibid.

20. Ibid., p. 109.

21. *The White Goddess: A Historical Grammar of Poetic Myth* (Ne York: Vintage Books, 1958), p. 124.

22. *Sun Lore of All Ages: A Collection of Myths and Legends Concer ing the Sun and Its Worship* (New York: G. P. Putnam's Sons, 1914 p. 230.

23. *Myth and Ritual in Christianity* (New York: Grove Press, Inc 1960), p. 87.

24. Sir James George Frazer, *The Golden Bough: A Study in Mag and Religion,* 1 vol., abridged ed. (New York: The Macmillan Co., 1951 p. 568.

25. *The Ancient Sun Kingdoms of the Americas* (Cleveland and Ne York: World Publishing Co., 1961), p. 98.

26. Alfonso Caso, *The Aztecs: People of the Sun,* trans. Lowell Dunha (Norman: University of Oklahoma Press, 1958), pp. 72–73.

27. Laurette Séjourné, *Burning Water: Thought and Religion in Ancie Mexico* (London and New York: Thames and Hudson, 1956), pp. 59–6

28. Caso, p. 73.

29. Séjourné, p. 152.

30. Frazer, *The Golden Bough,* p. 26.

31. *Firefly in the Night: A Study of Ancient Mexican Poetry and Sy bolism* (London: Faber and Faber, 1959), p. 187.

32. (New York: Harper and Brothers, 1958), pp. 88–89.

33. Séjourné, pp. 165–166.

CHAPTER SIX

The Duality of St. Mawr

IN HIS UNRESERVED PRAISE of "the astonishing work of genius that Lawrence's 'dramatic poem' is," F. R. Leavis declares, "'St. Mawr' seems to me to present a creative and technical originality not less remarkable than that of *The Waste Land,* and to be, more unquestionably than that poem, completely achieved, a full and self-sufficient creation."[1] To most other critics *St. Mawr* seems nothing of the sort.[2] But whatever the extravagance of Dr. Leavis's evaluation, his comparison between *St. Mawr* and *The Waste Land* is not itself inappropriate. Although his methods were different, D. H. Lawrence's problems were similar to T. S. Eliot's: to find symbols of sufficient sterility to embody the moral waste land of contemporary life and a myth potent enough to transform it. It is from the necessity imposed by these twin problems that *St. Mawr* derives its dual methods, social satire and myth.

1

In *St. Mawr,* as in eighteenth-century comedy, a conventionalized cast is the vehicle for social satire. Lawrence's symbol of the waste land is English society, from the horsemen and horsewomen of Hyde Park to the life of country houses and vicarages.

The chief target in Lawrence's attack on the affectations of this society is the effete, dilettante painter, Rico Carrington. In his stock characterization the mechanical, the petty, the artificial are always uppermost. Rico means it when he says, "Lou, dearest, *don't* spend a fortune on a horse for me, which I *don't* want. Honestly, I prefer a car" (p. 15). Lou comes to think of him as "poor old Rico, going on like an amiable machine from day to day" (p. 81). Rico reduces everyone to the diminutive: Lou is "Loulina," Flora Manby will become "Fiorita: or perhaps Florecita" (p. 101); thinking the world "a very queer one when Rico is the god Priapus," Lou tries to imagine the absurdity of "Sir Prippy" (pp. 103–104). Like Lawrence's other figures of the false artist, such as Sir Clifford Chatterley, Rico cares a great deal more for appearance than for reality. Thus, he is consistently defined and qualified by the metaphor of clothes. Appearing "all handsome and in the picture in white flannels with an apricot silk shirt," he looks ridiculous reprimanding the Indian servant Phoenix (p. 32). Before riding St. Mawr to Corrabach,

> he dressed himself most carefully in white riding-breeches and a shirt of purple silk crepe, with a flowing black tie spotted red like a ladybird, and black riding-boots. Then he took a *chic* little white hat with a black band. [p. 33]

Of this florid description, Graham Hough says:

> This is a grotesquely impossible get-up for even the most flower-like young man; but what is far more impossible is that Rico in this outfit should be admired and worshipped by the conventional hunting young woman Flora Manby. In reality she would never speak to a man who could be seen in such a costume.[3]

What is important, such criticism to the contrary, is not the possibilities of social behavior "in reality" but the satirical purpose of the overstatement, to attack the *un*reality of a society that accepts affectation as the norm. Rico, whose dress is studiedly anti-natural, is "becoming an almost fashionable portrait-painter" (p. 5). His vogue is dangerous, not because his portraits of society are unlikely to be more aesthetically pleasing than his self-decoration, but because his tastelessness reflects an urge that is really counter to nature and life. As Kingsley Widmer observes, with his "purple shirts, brocaded bed jacket, weird riding attire, along with his flirtacious but nonsexual relations with women and his supercilious affectations, Rico becomes the living symbol of emasculation used by Lawrence for harsh satire of modern sophisticated men."[4] The rise of the fop is proportionate to the decline of the phallic male. And what is dangerous about the false artist is that he is a false prophet.

Lawrence's stock characterization of Rico and his society has not been taken by some critics as satirical in purpose. The objections raised seem to me important matters for further exploration. Interestingly, both Hough and Eliseo Vivas employ imagery of the stage in asserting their view of the falsity of Lawrence's picture of English society. Hough complains that "this whole elaborately painted English scene is pure pasteboard, a stage set done with nothing deeper than a scene-painter's knowledge."[5] Vivas contends that Lawrence "had done it before and done it better":

Here we are witnessing another puppet show. Or rather, it is the old stock company again, and we know each and every one of the actors. The man now playing Rico is the same man who played Clifford Chatterley. . . . And Lou, playing now an American role, is Connie. . . . The groom is the man who played Mellors. . . .[6]

In his fine defense of *St. Mawr*, Alan Wilde has demonstrated that Hough's "description is accurate, but the complaint behind it is un-justified"[7] since Lou herself has the same feeling: "People, all the people she knew seemed so entirely contained within their cardboard let's-be-happy world" (p. 25). As she later puts it in a letter to her mother: "It is terrible when the life-flow dies out of one, and every-thing is like cardboard, and oneself is like cardboard" (p. 103). Vivas's complaint seems to me unjustified for similar reasons. In society Lou has the "quaint air of playing at being well bred, in a sort of charade game" (p. 3). In the country Mrs. Witt becomes a spectator at a performance: "Mrs. Witt had now a new pantomime to amuse her"; ". . . there she had the whole thing staged complete for her: English village life" (p. 27).

Too much concern with verisimilitude tends to obscure other valid considerations in art. Vivas's reference to *St. Mawr* as a puppet show calls to mind Lawrence's own remarks on the figures in the marionette show near the end of *Sea and Sardinia*:

There is something extremely suggestive in them. How much better they fit the old legend-tales than living people do. Nay, if we are going to have human beings on the stage, they should be masked and disguised. For in fact drama is enacted by symbolic creatures formed out of human conscious-ness: puppets if you like: but not human *individuals*. Our stage is all wrong, so boring in its personality. [p. 202]

Lawrence's fiction exists on several levels of abstraction, ranging from the particular to the general, from the realistic to the symbolic, from the representational to the presentational. The greater Lawrence's tendency toward higher levels of abstraction, as in such parables as

The Woman Who Rode Away and *The Man Who Died,* the more useful his discussion of the puppet figures becomes as a gloss on his method. The discussion is also relevant to Lawrence's unrealistic distortions of character in the satirical mode. Vivas, who declines to take sides against Sir Clifford Chatterley because he is "a mere name for a constellation of qualities that Lawrence hated," applies the same principle of judgment to Rico Carrington, "the arch-villain of *St. Mawr*—if a spiritual castrato can be called a villain."[8] This opinion is consistent with what one expects of a realistic novel: believable conflict involving not merely the clash of abstractions but also the encounter of persons: credible characters not merely being, in the sum of their stereotyped responses, artificial, changeless, predictable, but emerging instead in the emotional and moral ambiguities of life. But Rico, Sir Clifford Chatterley, and their Laurentian counterparts, moving in no such ambiguities, have become, in the emotional fixity of their neuroses and the moral fixity of their spiritual emptiness, little more than the mechanistic constellations of self-defeating stock responses. Lou Carrington, Connie Chatterley, and their Laurentian counterparts, on the other hand, in their emotional and moral viability, retain the potential of organic growth. The former, in their sterile inflexibility, remain in the static world of things; the latter, in their creative energy, evolve in the dynamic world of persons. The contrast in modes is between the closed system of satire and the open system of realism. Far from striving for novelistic verisimilitude, Lawrence, in his stock characterizations, is holding up to English society the steel glass of satire.

The satirical attack upon Rico is led by his mother-in-law, Mrs. Rachel Witt. As her name implies, her principal weapon is wit, the faculty of analytical intelligence by which she skeptically dissects seeming similitudes, finely discriminates between appearance and reality, and briskly dispatches her opponent with a lively riposte. Of Hyde Park's apparent friendliness she remarks: "So friendly! That's why I mistrust it so entirely—"(p. 20). Perhaps recalling her son-in-law's preference for outlandish neckwear, she distinguishes, in a comment on Lewis's refusal to shave off his beard, between the groom's genuine phallicism and Rico's mere display: "But, do you know it hadn't occurred to me that men wore their beards, like they wear their neckties, for show. I shall always remember Lewis for saying his beard was part of him" (pp. 21–22). She also notes the incongruity of Rico's riding St. Mawr. Deflating Rico's idle fancy that he may be created "Lord St. Mawr," she suggests the true meaning of lordship by retorting, "You mean . . . his real lordship would be the horse?" After maliciously making the stallion bolt with him, she dispatches Rico triumphantly with "We didn't get on very well with his lordship this morning" (pp. 22–23). In another discussion she makes a pointed contrast between Dean Vyner and Rico:

"You can't imagine his wife asking him to thread a needle. Something after all so *robust!* So different from *young* Englishmen, who all seem to me like ladies, perfect ladies."
"*Somebody* has to keep up the tradition of the perfect lady," said Rico.
"I know it," said Mrs. Witt. "And if the women won't do it, the young gentlemen take on the burden. They bear it very well." [p. 29]

Wit also takes the form of more extended verbal contests. In the ride to the Angel's Chair and the Devil's Chair Mrs. Witt's sardonic observation, "They give the Devil the higher seat in this country, do they? I think they're right," opens a Laurentian version of the debate between ancients and moderns, in which Lou and her mother side with the ancients against Rico, Fred Edwards, and Flora and Elsie Manby, who speak for the moderns. The setting, "one of those places where the spirit of aboriginal England still lingers," makes Lou feel that the present race has almost lasted too long: "All these millions of ancestors have used all the life up." When Edwards objects to the implication that the ancient devil worshippers were "better than we are," Lou replies, "We don't exist." Flora Manby prefers the present time because it is "the best age there ever was for a girl to have a good time in," an opinion supported by her reading of H. G. Wells's history. The final comment on the modern world, however, is left to St. Mawr. When Edwards begins to whistle a modern dance tune, the horse shies and rears until Rico pulls him "over backwards on top of him" (pp. 59–62).

This incident only endears St. Mawr further to Mrs. Witt, who, in a subsequent debate, defends him against the opinion of Dean and Mrs. Vyner that he should be destroyed. Recalling Rico's affectedly addressing her as "*belle-mère*," she refers to herself as a "bell-mare," not only punning on the sound but also making a "turn" on the thought, thereby rejecting the role of social object for identification with the instinctual being of the horse. By pointedly repeating the word "stallion" ten times, to the discomfort of the Vyners, she manages to suggest why St. Mawr must be saved (pp. 76–78). As she puts it more explicitly to Lou: "I'll preserve one last male thing in the museum of this world, if I can" (p. 84).

Whatever its satirical value, wit is not the whole of life for Lawrence but only one side of the dynamic polarity between creation and destruction. Repeatedly Lawrence asserts that the rhythm of history, of human psychology, and of art is dual. His theory of history is based on the idea that civilization develops by the alternating motives of peace and martial contest. His theory of psychology is rooted in the concept of polarized tension between the positive and negative functions of the psyche, the dynamic interchange between the lower sensual plane and the upper spiritual plane of consciousness. And his theory of classic American literature affirms that its quality derives from the dual rhythms of sloughing the old European consciousness and forming the new American consciousness underneath. Mrs. Witt's wit, however useful it may be in dispatching Rico, is a function only of the disintegrative, sundering vibration. That is, it is a function of analysis rather than synthesis, of will rather than blood, of mind rather than body. Usually associated with images of destruction, Mrs. Witt seems "to be pointing a pistol at the bosom of every other horseman and horsewoman and announcing: *Your virility or your life! Your femininity or your life!* " (p. 8). She insists on cutting Lewis's hair, while Lou, recognizing the threat of castration in the phallic woman's "terrifying shears with their beak erect," cries, "Not too short, mother, not too short!" (pp. 42–43). Taking a cottage in Shropshire overlooking the churchyard, Mrs. Witt remarks: "I never knew what a comfort it would be . . . to have grave-stones under my drawing-room windows, and funerals for lunch" (p. 26). She is described as a purely analytical "fiendish psychologist": "If anatomy presupposes a corpse, then psychology presupposes a world of corpses," the author observes, ". . . a whole world laboratory of human psyches waiting to be vivisected" (p. 28).

Since wit as intellectual analysis involves only one side of man's body-mind duality, Lou, in a debate on body and mind, must educate her mother in a larger concept of intelligence. The verbal contest takes the form of an extended anatomy of the word "mind." Declaring that "there's something else besides mind and cleverness," Lou suggests: "Perhaps it is the animal. Just think of St. Mawr! . . . We call him an animal, but we never know what it means. He seems a far greater mystery to me than a clever man." Mrs. Witt counters: "You won't tell me that the mere animal is all that counts in a man. I will never believe it. Man is wonderful because he is able to *think*." "But is he?" Lou demands. What exasperates Lou is the pettiness of most men's thinking: "all so childish: like stringing the same beads over and over again. Ah, men! They and their thinking are all so *paltry*. How can you be impressed?" Conceding the point, her mother replies sardonically: "Perhaps I'm not—any more." When Mrs. Witt characterizes such men as Dean Vyner as "old women knitting the same pattern over and over again," Lou raises the question: "But what is real mind? The old woman who knits the most complicated pattern?" (p. 45). Broadening the concept of "mind" to include instinctual as well as mental awareness, Lou turns again to the animal side of man's nature: "I believe Lewis has far more real mind than Dean Vyner or any of the clever ones. He has a good intuitive mind, he knows things without thinking them" (p. 46). The availability of intuition does not mean, however, that man can return to a primitive state. As Lawrence says of Melville's South Sea islanders, man has progressed too far in the "consciousness-struggle" to return to the uncreated past. Thus, when Mrs. Witt concludes, incredulously, that her daughter really wants "the cave man, who'll knock you on the head with a club," Lou replies:

"Don't be silly, mother. That's much more your subconscious line, you admirer of Mind—I don't consider the cave man is a real human animal at all. He's a brute, a degenerate. A pure animal man would be as lovely as a deer or a leopard, burning like a flame fed straight from underneath." [p. 47]

What Lou wants is a consciousness in man that still draws life from an instinctual and cosmic source. Thus, her definition of "mind" must encompass not only the disintegrative but the integrative vibration in a total life rhythm. As she concludes, "Ah, no, mother, I want the wonder back again, or I shall die. I don't want to be like you, just criticising and annihilating these dreary people, and enjoying it": "You enjoy shattering people like Dean Vyner. But I am young, I can't live that way!" (pp. 47–48).

2

The energy that could revive the waste-land society of Lawrence's satire is presented as mythic potential in the figure of the stallion St. Mawr. It will be helpful before evaluating the thematic function of St. Mawr to consider first the general mythic significance of the horse archetype and then the particular thematic function of the horse throughout Lawrence's work. In his analysis of the archetype as it occurs widely in mythology, folklore, and dreams, Carl G. Jung concludes that the horse "represents the non-human psyche, the subhuman, animal side, the unconscious. . . . As an animal lower than man it represents the lower part of the body and the animal impulses that rise from there."[9] The horse in Lawrence's work usually connotes the instinctual life of the body. In such short stories as "Strike Pay" and "The Horse Dealer's Daughter," horses seem to represent the spirit of man that is crushed by society. In "The Horse Dealer's Daughter," in fact, horses are presented as stupid, subjugated creatures. In "The Blind Man" the horses are equated with living, palpable darkness, the unseeing, unknowing, instinctual world which Maurice Pervin inhabits in his blindness. In both *The Princess* and *The Woman Who Rode Away* horses, as the means of transport from one realm of being to another, define the nature of the heroines' quests. In "The Rocking Horse Winner," the horse is reduced to the service of Mammon as Paul's instinctual being is sacrificed, in the complex autoerotic metaphor of riding the hobby horse,[10] to meet the demands of the mother's lust for money. In the novels the horse is an even more striking symbol. In the last chapter of *The Rainbow*, Ursula's encounter with the horses marks a turn in her life from the pretensions of society and the mechanistic, destructive sexuality of Skrebensky and a movement toward the free, instinctual life. In *Women in Love*, Gerald Crich's subduing of the Arabian mare at the train is a graphic presentation of the subjugation of instinctual being by modern will, a symbolic parallel to the breaking of the miners' spirit by the industrial society which Gerald represents. In the introductory chapter of *The Plumed Serpent*, the broken horses of the bullring, gored in the vitals from behind, represent the dark consciousness sodomized by the modern white consciousness in the sterile thrill of degraded sexuality.

Lawrence learned to ride horseback, by Mabel Dodge Luhan's account, in New Mexico. Although his awkwardness at first made Tony Luhan laugh, he soon became an accomplished rider:

He was absolutely fearless and he never fell off, no matter what the horse did. Though he was unaccustomed to riding, he took to it naturally and easily, though he always looked uncomfortable on horseback, bent over forward and riding as though the saddle hurt him. He rode with a very free rein. Fast. He couldn't endure to have me go ahead of him across the fields. . . . I suppose he simply couldn't stand the idea of a woman in the lead.[11]

Subsequently, the horse becomes an even more complex and explicit symbol for Lawrence. In New Mexico Lawrence was an occasional contributor to *Laughing Horse* magazine. His design for No. 16, which Willard Johnson says was not used, shows a rather phallic stallion pursuing a mare.[12] Two of Lawrence's expository statements on the horse have special relevance to the reading of *St. Mawr*.

The first, his letter to Johnson on 9 January 1924 in response to Johnson's sending him the *Laughing Horse* magazine, contains the germ of the short novel. The conflict between the sensual, pagan world of St. Mawr and Lewis and the sterile, spiritualized world of Rico, Dean Vyner, and Flora Manby is hinted at in Lawrence's opinion that "over here the Horse is dead: he'll kick his heels no more. I don't know whether it's the pale Galilean who has triumphed, or a paleness paler even than the pallor of Jesus." Foreshadowing his fusion in the figure of St. Mawr of the centaur and Pan, Lawrence declares:

Two-legged man is no good. If he's going to stand steady, he must stand on four feet. Like the Centaur. When Jesus was born, the spirits wailed around the Mediterranean: *Pan is dead. Great Pan is dead.* And at the Renaissance the Centaur gave a final groan, and expired.

But Lawrence is already looking forward to their resurrection: "It would be a terrible thing if the horse in us died for ever, as he seems to have died in Europe." Deriding the modern tendency to reduce the horse to a mere sign, Lawrence enumerates four specific functions of the centaur, which he was to embody in the figure of St. Mawr:

In modern symbolism, the Horse is supposed to stand for the passions. Passions be blowed. What does the Centaur stand for. . . . That's the blue Horse of the ancient Mediterranean, before the pale Galilean or the extrapale German or Nordic gentleman conquered. First of all, Sense, Good Sense, Sound Sense, Horse Sense. And then, a laugh, a loud, sensible Horse Laugh. After that, these same passions, glossy and dangerous in the flanks. And after these again, hoofs, irresistible, splintering hoofs, that can kick the walls of the world down.

Horse-sense, Horse-laughter, Horse-passion, Horse-hoofs: ask the Indians if it is not so.

Lawrence's conception of the horse as archetype is summarized in *Apocalypse*, written in the year before he died:

How the horse dominated the mind of the early races, especially of the Mediterranean! You were a lord if you had a horse. Far back, far back in our dark soul the horse prances. He is a dominant symbol: he gives us lord-

ship: he links us, the first palpable and throbbing link with the ruddy-glow-
ing Almighty of potence: he is the beginning even of our godhead in the
flesh. And as a symbol he roams the dark underworld meadows of the soul.
He stamps and threshes in the dark fields of your soul and of mine. The sons
of God who came down and knew the daughters of men and begot the great
Titans, they had "the members of horses," says Enoch.

Within the last fifty years man has lost the horse. Now man is lost. Man
is lost to life and power—an underling and a wastrel. While horses thrashed
the streets of London, London lived.

The horse, the horse! the symbol of surging potency and power of movement, of action, in man. [pp. 97–98]

In tracing the horse as a dynamic figure in man's consciousness to its
primordial sources in religious and sexual mystery Lawrence converts
the image from fixed allegorical sign to archetypal symbol. As he distinguishes between the two kinds of image in *Apocalypse*: "Allegory
can always be explained: and explained away. The true symbol defies
all explanation, so does the true myth. . . . Because symbol and myth
do not affect us only mentally, they move the deep emotional centres
every time" (pp. 183–184). The fixed sign, the reduction of the whole
to a single part, Lawrence rejects: "When as a small boy I learnt from
Euclid that: 'The whole is greater than the part,' I immediately knew
that that solved the problem of allegory for me" (p. 8). Distinguishing
between the mental logic of allegory and the intuitive logic of symbolism, he echoes Saint Paul: "The mind knows in part, in part and
parcel, with full stop after every sentence. But the emotional soul
knows in full, like a river or a flood" (p. 184). Lawrence affirms a
mode of knowing that is anterior to classical culture: "It was a great
depth of knowledge arrived at direct, by instinct and intuition, as we
say, not by reason. It was a knowledge based not on words but on
images. The abstraction was not into generalisations or into qualities,
but into symbols" (p. 76).

In his short novel, Lawrence's expanding conceptions of the horse,
the centaur, and Pan coalesce in the dynamic symbol of St. Mawr.
The reiterated image of the centaur attributes to horse and rider a
mythic unity. If Phoenix looks "as if he and the horse were all in one
piece" (p. 19), Lewis seems "to sink himself in the horse" so remark-
ably that Mrs. Witt declares: "When I speak to him, I'm not sure
whether I'm speaking to a man or to a horse" (p. 22). Even Rico,
riding St. Mawr to Corrabach, can feel himself "a hero from another,
heroic world" (p. 34). Of greater significance for St. Mawr's world-
generative role are images of the "Pan-cluster." Patricia Merivale,

who sees "Pan in America" as Lawrence's manifesto for the period, says that in *St. Mawr* he "adapts the material of the essay to novelistic purposes." Confronted with a world full of "fallen Pans," men who, "however much they may *look* like the goat-god, have in fact been defeated by man's original Fall into consciousness,"[13] Lou turns to St. Mawr as the incarnation of prelapsarian phallic mystery. The other human characters as well are consistently measured by the quality of their responses to him as god-beast. A discussion of Pan turns inevitably to the contrast between St. Mawr and the "fallen Pans." Cartwright, who superficially resembles the god, believes that "Pan once was a great god before the anthropomorphic Greeks turned him into half a man." Dean Vyner thinks that "the world will always be full of goaty old satyrs," but he finds them "somewhat vulgar." Mrs. Witt muses pointedly, "Wouldn't a man be wonderful in whom Pan hadn't fallen!" When she asks her daughter, "Did you ever see Pan in a man, as you see Pan in St. Mawr?" Lou replies, "I see—mostly—a sort of—pancake" (pp. 50–52). Man as pancake is represented by the young men of Rico's social set, who strike Lou as "handsome, young, bare-faced unrealities, not men at all" (p. 25). It is, therefore, fitting that St. Mawr should not only injure the Oedipal Rico's foot but also kick young Edwards in his bare face, leaving him disfigured (p. 62). In view of St. Mawr's identification with the pagan deity it is ironically appropriate that Dean Vyner is the one to say: "We all know, Mrs. Witt, that the author of the mischief is St. Mawr himself" (p. 77).

As a mythic symbol St. Mawr fulfills one of the essential functions of mythology, as Joseph Campbell defines it, "that of eliciting and supporting a sense of awe before the mystery of being."[14] John B. Vickery calls the stallion a totemic animal,[15] but a totem, in the terms of Sir James George Frazer's anthropology, "is never an isolated individual but always a class of objects, generally a species of animals or plants. . . ."[16] Although there is respect for the horse as the species in which the phallic mystery survives, genuine reverence is reserved almost exclusively for St. Mawr. St. Mawr is, I believe, an incarnation of the transcendent and immanent mystery of being. This mythic construct is discussed instructively by Campbell: "In the sacred books of the Orient, the ultimate mystery of being is said to be transcendent, in the sense that it 'transcends' (lies above or beyond) human knowledge, thought, sight, and speech. However, since it is explicitly identified with the mystery of our own being, and of all being whatsoever, it is declared to be immanent as well. . . ."[17] The transcendence of St.

Mawr's mystery is expressed, for example, in Lou's observation: "We call him an animal, but we never know what it means. He seems a far greater mystery to me than a clever man" (p. 45). Yet the immanence of this mystery in the cosmos is made evident in St. Mawr's luminous existence in contrast to the unreality of men in the waste land. Burning, like Blake's "tyger," with "dark invisible fire" (p. 11), the stallion is transfigured for Lou into pagan divinity. In the epiphany she recognizes in St. Mawr the possibility of escape from the personal crisis into which her marriage to Rico has led her: "In his dark eye, that looked with its cloudy brown pupil, a cloud within a dark fire, like a world beyond our world, there was a dark vitality glowing, and within the fire another sort of wisdom" (p. 25). The brilliance of Lawrence's achievement in the numen of St. Mawr is illustrated in Campbell's discussion of "the characteristic mental state of all religion," the "recognition of the *numinous*":

It is, on the primitive level, demonic dread; on the highest, mystical rapture; and between there are many grades. Defined, it may be talked about and taught; but talk and teaching cannot produce it. Nor can authority enforce it. Only the accident of experience and the sign symbols of a living myth can elicit and support it; but such signs cannot be invented. They are found. Whereupon they function of themselves. And those who find them are the sensitized, creative, living minds that once were known as seers, but now as poets and creative artists. More important, more effective for the future of a culture than its statesmen or its armies are these masters of the spiritual breath by which the clay of man wakes to life.[18]

If St. Mawr is animal and god, Morgan Lewis is his priest and Druidism the ritual of his invocation. The syncretism of Lawrence's mythical method, the concept that all gods share in the mythic identity of the cosmos but manifest themselves separately and locally, allows an equine divinity, derived out of Welsh stock by the Mediterranean Pan, to be approached through Celtic religion. Although clearly one of Lawrence's small, bearded ego-figures who moves comfortably in "the darkness of the old Pan" (p. 95), the groom, unlike the major characters of The Plumed Serpent, is the servant of divinity rather than its incarnation. On his initial appearance, Lewis is grooming St. Mawr "with an absorption that was almost ritualistic." As Lou explains: "He goes with the horse. . . . If we buy St. Mawr we get the man thrown in" (p. 16). On their ride through the dark forest, Lewis tells Mrs. Witt the Celtic fairy lore of his boyhood when children ate the flying ash seeds called pigeons to become "moon-boys": "If you want to matter, you must become a moon-boy. Then all your life, fire can't blind you, and people can't hurt you" (p. 96). The identification of St. Mawr with pagan deity, already established in the Pan imagery, is strengthened by allusions to ancient British folklore. The ash, according to Robert Graves a tree of rebirth, is sacred to Gwydion, a Teuton-Celt deity equated with Woden. Significantly for *St. Mawr*, the Norse name of Gwydion's horse was "*Askr Yggr-drasill,* or Ygdrasill, 'the ash-tree that is the horse of Yggr,' Yggr being one of Woden's titles."[19] Lewis seems to Mrs. Witt "to inhabit another world than hers. A world dark and still, where language never ruffled the growing leaves and seared their edges like a bad wind" (p. 92). The setting of this scene, allusive with oak and ash, falling star and demonic moonlight, suggests an ancient cosmic order anterior to words. As Geoffrey Bibby describes the religion of the eleventh century B.C. "Celtic dawn":

[The Celtic] gods were not the gods of the open spaces and the open heavens, the sun-god and the wind-gods and the god of thunder; they were not even, as one might have expected, farmer deities, corn spirits and fertility goddesses. No, these Celts worshipped older gods (somehow, one knew that they were older), gods of the forest and the hunt, gods with deer antlers or with three faces, gods who lived in oak trees and in the mistletoe, gods that were worshipped by moonlight.[20]

Following his usual practice, Lawrence makes ironic use of the Christian tradition that the gods of the pagan world are devils in disguise. Lewis, in a Laurentian, pagan sense, is being deeply religious but, in a Christian sense, subversive when he tells Mrs. Witt, "I never said I didn't believe in God.—Only I'm sure I'm not a Methodist" (p. 91). Rico, conversely, is speaking in a Christian frame of reference when he calls St. Mawr "accursed" (p. 54). Lawrence's point is succinctly stated in the Devil's Chair scene in Mrs. Witt's observation: "They give the Devil the higher seat in this country, do they?" (p. 59).

When Rico, predictably, concludes that St. Mawr should be shot as a dangerous animal, Lou demands, "And do you think we ought to shoot everything that is dangerous?" (p. 74). But what the sterile Rico finally plans for St. Mawr is a meaner betrayal than death: a dying god can remain a potent force; a castrated god cannot. Rico determines to sell the stallion to Flora Manby, one of Lawrence's flower-picking types, who wants him gelded. Lou despairs of "our whole eunuch civilisation, nasty-minded as eunuchs are, with their

kind of sneaking, sterilising cruelty." Her mother acidly advises her to
tell Flora: " 'Miss Manby, you may have my husband, but not my
horse. My husband won't need emasculating, and my horse I won't
have you meddle with.' " Mrs. Witt and Lou quite literally "preserve
one last male thing in the museum of this world" (p. 84) by spiriting
St. Mawr away to America.

The conclusion of the short novel, in which Lou leaves St. Mawr in
Texas and moves on to a lone existence on Las Chivas ranch in New
Mexico, has caused much dissatisfaction among critics. Father
William Tiverton thinks the narrative "bi-valvular" because St. Mawr
is dropped from the story two-thirds of the way through.[21] Vivas dis-
cerns an apparent failure in coherence between the English and New
Mexican parts of the story.[22] And Anthony Beal scoffs that St. Mawr
winds up on a Texas dude ranch, "ignominiously sniffing round after
the owner's mare: the symbol of all Lawrence's positives is come to
this!"[23]

The changes in setting and symbol, however, are both dramatically
motivated and thematically consistent. Through apocalyptic imagery,
Lawrence has prepared the way for a new beginning. Lewis, seeing a
falling star, tells Mrs. Witt: "There's movement in the sky. The world
is going to change again." Rejecting her scientific explanation of such
phenomena, he believes that "stones don't come at us from the sky for
nothing" (p. 97). Lou and Mrs. Witt, crossing the Atlantic with St.
Mawr, have a "queer, transitory, unreal feeling": "Never again to see
the mud and snow of a northern winter, nor to feel the idealistic,
Christianised tension of the now irreligious North" (p. 117). Alan
Wilde calls Las Chivas, the New Mexican ranch where Lou ends her
journey, "bedrock," where the story ends "in anticipation of the reborn
society, the phallic millennium."[24]

3

The phallic millennium, however, though inherent in the "wild
spirit" of the western landscape, is not yet ushered in. For Mrs. Witt
the revelation of St. Mawr comes too late. Already identified with
death, the negative principle that informs her wit, she moves from the
English cottage overlooking the churchyard to the isolation of her
New Mexican hotel room. For her the quality of living is to be
measured by the quality of dying. She asks, "Oh, Death, where is thy
sting-a-ling-a-ling?" For the modern world, in its diminution even of
dying, has rendered living meaningless: "I want death to be real to

me. . . . If it hurts me enough, I shall know I was alive" (pp. 79–80). In America she tells Lou, "I have come home to die" (p. 123). Neither Lewis nor Phoenix can usher in the new world. Lewis serves the mystery of St. Mawr and, recognizing his own priestly function as well as Mrs. Witt's destructive one, wisely rejects her proposal of marriage (pp. 98–100). Phoenix, whose rodent sexuality is all that remains of the phallic potential in him, is "ready to trade his sex, which, in his opinion, every white woman was secretly pining for, for the white woman's money and social privileges" (pp. 125–126). Lou, recognizing his motives for what they are, becomes a Vestal Virgin, "weary of the embrace of incompetent men, . . . turning to the unseen gods, the unseen spirits, the hidden fire, and devoting herself to that, and that alone" (p. 128).

Near the end of *The Waste Land*, Eliot's speaker turns his back on the "arid plain" and, fishing on the shore, asks: "Shall I at least set my lands in order?" (ll. 423–425). Lawrence's position is similar to Eliot's but goes further:

What's to be done? Generally speaking, nothing. The dead will have to bury their dead, while the earth stinks of corpses. The individual can but depart from the mass, and try to cleanse himself. . . . Retreat to the desert, and fight. But in his soul adhere to that which is life itself, creatively destroying as it goes: destroying the stiff old thing to let the new bud come through. [pp. 66–67]

In the unregenerate waste land of modern civilization the heroic quest becomes the ordering of one's own values. Wilde perceptively defends Lawrence's ending to *St. Mawr* by suggesting that "however little action there is in the novel, the curve it describes . . . . indicates . . . the progress of Lou from confusion and from immersion in the social world of her husband to a state of solitary self-knowledge."[25]

St. Mawr, some critical opinion to the contrary, disappears from the story only after he has fulfilled his function as curative symbol for Lou. In her despair of finding phallic potential in the two-dimensional men of her social world she has begun to feel herself a figure of cardboard. The advent of St. Mawr establishes a significant alternative to the sterile non-existence which characterizes modern society. The expansion of Lou's consciousness, which begins with this epiphany, does not end there. The symbolic realization which St. Mawr brings to Lou leads her, first, to the desperate impression of overwhelming evil flooding the earth, then, to the practical decision to reject her meaningless marriage in the waste land for the lonely but satisfying vision of cosmic being at Las Chivas. If Rico chooses to join her there, a possibility which Lou is still reluctant to contemplate, it will not be on the terms of their old sterile relationship: she will not *"bring* him" (p. 143). Her moral crisis resolved, Lou no longer requires the symbolic godhead of St. Mawr for continued realization of the mystery of being. To reify the stallion in that role would be, in fact, a sort of idolatry involving mechanical manipulation of the static sign rather than organic experience of the living symbol. One index to Lou's maturation is that, rather than becoming fixated at one stage of development, she is able to relinquish even the source of her inspiration to the fulfillment of his own instinctual being and to continue her own creative growth in the life newly opened to her. St. Mawr's meaning, at once intensely physical and intensely religious, is abstracted at Las Chivas as the spirit of the place. This "wild spirit," which it is the purpose of a long digression to define, dominates the history of the goat ranch. Like Shelley's west wind, it is both "destroyer and preserver," defeating all attempts to bend its inhuman force to the civilizing will, yet inspiriting the land with myriad life. It is to this fierce spirit that Lou now must turn in service. Wilde is willing to concede that Lou's talk of the wild spirit's wanting, needing, and craving for her "provides the one absolutely false note in the novel."[26] But the love to which Lawrence is referring is neither romantic nor Christian love. The ranch, on the contrary, is "a world before and after the God of Love" (p. 139), a prelapsarian condition informed by the tension between positive and negative impulses which makes wholeness and growth possible. The wild spirit needs Lou for the creative evolution of the new order. Lawrence's conclusion is an affirmation which, it seems to me, he has earned.

NOTES

1. *D. H. Lawrence: Novelist* (New York: Alfred A. Knopf, 1956), p. 279.

2. Several adverse criticisms will be considered in the following pages. The reader may also wish to consult Robert Liddell, "Lawrence and Dr. Leavis: The Case of *St. Mawr*," *Essays in Criticism,* IV (July, 1954), 321–327, a negative reaction which is answered by David Craig, Mark Roberts, and T. W. Thomas in the "Critical Forum" of *Essays in Criticism,* V (January, 1955), 64–80.

3. Graham Hough, *The Dark Sun: A Study of D. H. Lawrence* (New York: The Macmillan Co., 1957), pp. 182–183.

4. *The Art of Perversity: D. H. Lawrence's Shorter Fictions* (Seattle: University of Washington Press, 1962), pp. 70–71.

5. Hough, p. 183.

6. Eliseo Vivas, *D. H. Lawrence: The Failure and the Triumph of Art* (London: George Allen and Unwin Ltd., 1961), pp. 155–156. Vivas refers to the works in the order in which he considers them in his book rather than in the order of their publication.

7. Alan Wilde, "The Illusion of St. Mawr: Technique and Vision in D. H. Lawrence's Novel," *PMLA*, LXXIX (March, 1964), 165.

8. Vivas, p. 151.

9. "The Practical Use of Dream-Analysis," in *The Practice of Psychotherapy: Essays on the Psychology of the Transference and Other Subjects*, 2d ed. rev., The Bollingen Series XX (New York: Pantheon Books, Inc., 1966), p. 159.

10. See Neil D. Isaacs, "The Autoerotic Metaphor in Joyce, Sterne, Lawrence, Stevens, and Whitman," *Literature and Psychology*, XV (Spring, 1965), 92–106.

11. *Lorenzo in Taos* (New York: Alfred A. Knopf, 1932), pp. 76–77.

12. The design is reproduced in Harry T. Moore, *The Intelligent Heart: The Story of D. H. Lawrence* (New York: Farrar, Straus, and Young, Inc., 1954), after p. 308. Although Moore identifies the drawing as the cover design for No. 26, he learned subsequently that it was intended for No. 16, the number having been covered by a strip pasted over the original. Edward Nehls, ed., *D. H. Lawrence: A Composite Biography*, II (Madison: University of Wisconsin Press, 1958), pp. 500–503, n131, gives Moore's account of the design as well as a brief history of *Laughing Horse* by Willard Johnson and a bibliography of Lawrence's contributions to the magazine.

13. "D. H. Lawrence and the Modern Pan Myth," *Texas Studies in Literature and Language*, VI (1964), 301.

14. Joseph Campbell, *The Masks of God: Occidental Mythology* (New York: The Viking Press, 1964), p. 519.

15. "Myth and Ritual in the Shorter Fiction of D. H. Lawrence," *Modern Fiction Studies*, V (Spring, 1959), 79.

16. *Totemism and Exogamy: A Treatise on Certain Early Forms of Superstition and Society*, 4 vols. (London: Macmillan and Co., Ltd., 1935), I, 3–4.

17. *The Masks of God: Occidental Mythology,* p. 109.

18. Ibid., p. 519.

19. *The White Goddess: A Historical Grammar of Poetic Myth* (New York: Vintage Books, 1958), pp. 172, 44–45.

20. *Four Thousand Years Ago: A World Panorama of Life in the Second Millennium* B.C. (New York: Alfred A. Knopf, 1956), p. 374.

21. *D. H. Lawrence and Human Existence* (London: Rockliff, 1951), p. 75.

22. Vivas, p. 151.

23. *D. H. Lawrence* (Edinburgh and London: Oliver and Boyd, 1961), p. 101.

24. Wilde, pp. 167–168.

25. Ibid., p. 164.

26. Ibid., p. 169.

CHAPTER SEVEN

The Symbolic Structure of The Plumed Serpent

D. H. LAWRENCE attempts in *The Plumed Serpent* (1926), his major work of the period, the reconciliation of a series of paired opposites, presented on ascending levels of abstraction from the personal to the cosmic. As H. M. Daleski suggests, the most striking thing about Lawrence's world view is its dualism. While essentially agreeing with Henry Miller's opinion that "'Phoenix, Crown, Rainbow, Plumed Serpent, all these symbols centre about the same obsessive idea: *the resolution of two opposites in the form of a mystery*,'" Daleski thinks the word "resolution" misleading in that it implies "dissolution of the opposites": "Lawrence repeatedly insists that the parts retain their identity, that they are not neutralized in the process."[1] Daleski finds support for this important qualification in an instructive passage from *Twilight in Italy*, in which Lawrence affirms both the Self and Selflessness as the "twofold approach to God." Though "eternally separate," the sensual and the spiritual must be maintained in the equal balance of polar opposition, a relationship symbolized in the Holy Ghost of the Christian Trinity, which Lawrence identifies as "the relation that is established between the two Infinites, the two natures of God, which we have transgressed, forgotten, sinned against" (pp. 57–59). *The Plumed Serpent* was intended, I believe, as an invocation of the wholeness of the Holy Ghost.

First, the major thematic contrast of the novel is between a dissolute modern world characterized by societal dependence upon mechanical forms and individual enslavement to surface sensation, and a postulated world characterized by societal reliance upon organic forms and individual affirmation through instinctual being.

Second, this thematic contrast gives rise to the "double motive" of the novel, as Mary Freeman puts it, "on the one hand to explore for the European those modes of living that he had so carefully denied, and on the other, to suggest a move toward an indigenous Mexican renaissance."[2]

Third, this "double motive" is specified in a dual narrative movement. As Graham Hough observes, "there are really two plots": Kate's *Bildungsroman*, her "progress from one mode of life to another"— though rather than uniform forward motion, the "movement is one of oscillation, and the needle has not ceased to tremble at the end"; and "the whole story of the Quetzalcoatl movement," which, interwoven with the first plot, "is intended to provide an explanation of the changes that are going on in Kate's nature, the way her sympathy flows and recoils."[3]

Fourth, this dual narrative movement requires the form of two mythic patterns. For the first plot, as Jascha Kessler suggests, Lawrence employs the "separation—initiation—return" pattern of the monomyth. Though the ritual is not completed by Kate's return, her story does comprise, as Kessler says, the first two parts of the formula.[4] For the second plot, Lawrence uses the mythic pantheon of Toltec and Aztec gods of pre-Columbian Mexico, informed, as William York Tindall shows, by the astrology of Frederick Carter and the theosophy of Mme. H. P. Blavatsky.[5]

Fifth, this duo-mythic pattern, through the metaphorical function of contrasting characters, is employed in differentiating between white consciousness and dark consciousness as opposite modes of being. The effect of the contrast, however, rather than to reconcile the two, is to elevate the latter at the expense of the former. Thus, in unequally matched pairs, Don Ramón Carrasco and General Cipriano Viedma are the dark foils of the white Owen Rhys and Bud Villiers; Ramón's second wife, Teresa, is the dark opposite of his first wife, Carlota; Ramón, as leader of the dark religion of Quetzalcoatl, finds his reverse counterpart in the Bishop, the leader of the white religion of Christ. In further complication of the design, characters within each category are compared in degree. Villiers is colder, thus "whiter," than Rhys. Cipriano and Juana, as Indians, are naturalistically dark, whereas Ramón and Teresa are ideally dark. Cipriano, despite, or perhaps because of, his early chastity, is both more overtly phallic and more given to blood violence than the more spiritualized Ramón. As the disparity between white consciousness and dark consciousness becomes increasingly evident, Kate Leslie, as the focal character of the novel, oscillates, in Hough's term, in progressively narrowing circles toward the center of dark consciousness, the dark sun. The fact that her oscillation has not ceased at the end is a note of realism in a novel that is chiefly romance.

1

Since character is subordinated to symbolic structure, values in the novel are presented principally through the counters of image, incident, and ritual. Color imagery most immediately reveals the disparity between white and dark consciousness. On her fortieth birthday, Kate reflects that "the first half of her life was over. The bright page with its flowers and its love and its stations of the Cross ended with a grave. Now she must turn over, and the page was black, black and empty" (p. 45). Kate has sat, with Rhys and Villiers, at the bullfight in "reserved seats in the 'Sun'" (p. 1), where she has been revolted by the display, both in the bullring and in the stands, of sensation for the sake of sensation. But she has also shivered in the brooding darkness of Mrs. Norris's massive house in Tlacolula, a symbol of death willed to Mexico by the white conquistadores: "The square, inner patio, dark, with sun lying on the heavy arches of one side, had pots of red and white flowers, but was ponderous, as if dead for centuries." The flowers, in their balance of red and white, as well as the funereal but phallic "Aztec cypresses rising to strange dark heights" (pp. 26–27), suggest, in the characteristic ambiguity of Laurentian imagery, both the violence and death of Mexico and the life forces, inherent if unrealized, by which it could be revived. Similarly in the plaza in Mexico City the "sparkle of bright air" is a spiritual potential amid the deadness of "old roof surfaces," and the resulting counterpoint of life and death leads to the ambiguity of "the dark undertone, the black, serpent-like fatality all the time" (pp. 44–45).

As Kate is drawn gradually into the Quetzalcoatl movement, this "black, serpent-like fatality" is objectified in the central symbol of the novel, the dark sun. Perhaps unconsciously echoing Whitman's line: "The bright suns I see and the dark suns I cannot see are in their places' (*Song of Myself*, section 16, line 24), Lawrence presents the dark sun as the physical source of the spiritual energy of the bright sun: "Behind the fierce sun the dark eyes of a deeper sun were watching, and between the bluish ribs of the mountains a powerful heart was secretly beating, the heart of the earth" (p. 105). This "deeper sun" of blood consciousness appears, with the same color imagery, as a religious symbol on the banner of Quetzalcoatl: "On the blue field of

the banneret was the yellow sun with a black centre, and between the
four greater yellow rays, four black rays emerging, so that the sun
looked like a wheel spinning with a dazzling motion" (p. 116). The
flag combines the blue of the sky and the black of the earth, Quetzalcoatl's spiritual component of fidelity and his physical component
of instinctual blood consciousness. The dark sun, as source of creative
energy, is the life-generative force. As the old man of Quetzalcoatl, in
his sermon in the plaza at Sayula, relates the myth of creation:

". . . one of the gods with hidden faces . . . . looked up at the sun, and
through the sun he saw the dark sun, the same that made the sun and the
world, and will swallow it again like a draught of water.
    "He said: *Is it time?* And from the bright sun the four dark arms of the
greater sun shot out, and in the shadow men arose. They could see the four
dark arms of the sun in the sky. And they started walking." [pp. 118–119]

But despite this creative power of the dark sun, man turned away
from its chief prophet, Quetzalcoatl:

"So he cried to the Master-Sun, the dark one, of the unuttered name: I
am withering white like a perishing gourd-vine. I am turning to bone. I am
denied of these Mexicans. I am waste and weary and old. Take me away.
    "Then the dark sun reached an arm, and lifted Quetzalcoatl into the sky.
And the dark sun beckoned with a finger, and brought white men out of
the east. And they came with a dead god on the Cross, saying: Lo! This is
the Son of God! He is dead, he is bone! Lo, your god is bled and dead, he
is bone." [p. 120]

Quetzalcoatl departed, the old man explains, because he was betrayed
by men who turned from his religious principle of dark, instinctual
being, taming "the snakes of their body" by will, which is equated
throughout the novel with whiteness, and degenerating, as a result,
from blood consciousness to blood lust (p. 120). Laurette Séjourné,
a distinguished archaeologist who has made extensive excavations at
Teotihuacan, interprets the betrayal of Quetzalcoatl politically. The
concept of human sacrifice to replenish the sun is itself the degenerate
form of an earlier spiritual ideal: "The exalted revelation of the
eternal unity of the spirit was converted into a principle of cosmic
anthropophagy. . . . As seems usual in despotic systems, the Aztec
state was founded on a spiritual inheritance which it betrayed and
transformed into a weapon of worldly power."[6] Lawrence, on the other
hand, interprets the betrayal psychologically: "And when they could

not bear the fire of the sun, they said: The sun is angry. He wants to drink us up. Let us give him blood of victims" (p. 120). The spiritual energy of light has whitened into a repressive force which has diverted the instinctual energy of darkness from creative being to destructive perversion. The Mexicans, having acquired a white will, are ready for Christ, whom Lawrence presents as the white man's god of death. With the rebirth of Quetzalcoatl in the person of Ramón, however, the energy of darkness and the energy of light are both restored to their normal function. The two suns, though revolving in different directions, as symbolized in the counter motions of the inner and outer circles of the dance of the men and women of Quetzalcoatl, revolve in a harmonious pattern. With this integration of the sensual and the spiritual, creative being becomes possible. Susanne K. Langer's comments on dance are relevant to Lawrence's double circle dance:

Because dance-gesture is symbolic, objectified, every dance which is to have balletic significance primarily for the people engaged in it is necessarily ecstatic. It must take the dancer "out of himself," and it may do this by an astounding variety of means: . . . most primitive and natural of all—by weaving the "magic circle" round the altar or the deity, whereby every dancer is exalted at once to the status of a mystic. His every motion becomes dance-gesture because he has become a spirit, a dance-personage. . . .[7]

When a dark man leads Kate "toward the inner fire" of the dance, she is mystically renewed as "a virgin again, a young virgin." Kate sees in the lowered, abstracted faces of the dancers "the greater, not the lesser sex" (pp. 125–127).

For all her symbolic realization, however, Kate finds in the actual world that some problems persist. Though she is wheeled, as in the dance, toward the dark inner sun, the bright outer sun, in its counter motion, also plays its light upon her. She feels that "these men wanted to take her *will* away from her, as if they wanted to deny her the light of day" (p. 182). Sometimes when Kate's will diverts her from the greater to the lesser sexuality, she desires "the white ecstasy of frictional satisfaction." But when she forgoes "conscious 'satisfaction,'" "what happened was dark and untellable." In this distinction between manipulative gratification and instinctual communion in the orgasm, Lawrence marks the shift from light to dark, from the mechanical to the organic mode of being. Though Kate is still sometimes "Aphrodite of the foam" (p. 421), she is becoming Malintzi of the

green leaves. As such she can counter Cipriano-Huitzilopochtli's blood
sacrifice with redemptive pardon and rebirth, a contrast in function
signaled in their second meeting by Kate's insistence that she "would
like to give them hope" and Cipriano's stated opinion that "they have
some other strength, perhaps" (p. 34). This "other strength," for Cipriano, who evolves fittingly from general of the army to war god, lies
in the blood, as suggested by his liturgical color, red, and, if need be,
in blood sacrifice, as suggested by his color black. Kate's renewed virginity is connoted in the white dress and yellow shawl that she wears
in the opening of the Church of Quetzalcoatl in Sayula, where she
presents a striking contrast to Carlota, whose very name is historically
despised in Mexico as a symbol of white repression. In the scene in
the church her black dress, hysterical behavior, and death suggest the
"last station of the Cross" of white consciousness (pp. 333–350).

2

The disparity between white consciousness and dark consciousness,
signaled in the imagery, is further established by incident. Contrasting attitudes in the two modal worlds toward the counters of
violence and nakedness provide insight into the distinction Lawrence
makes between sensation and being—the distinction, that is, between
blood lust and blood consciousness.

The "grotesque and effeminate [matadors] in tight, ornate clothes
. . . . with their rather fat posteriors and their squiffs of pigtails" (p.
8) are effectively contrasted with the lean, masculine Cipriano when,
as Huitzilopochtli in his role of executioner, he stands "stripped of his
blanket, his body . . . painted in horizontal bars of red and black,
while from his mouth went a thin green line, and from his eyes a band
of yellow" (p. 370). The matadors practice "human cowardice and
beastliness" (p. 10) in torturing the bulls and allowing the horses to
be gored, whereas Cipriano "swift as lightning . . . stabbed the blind-
folded men to the heart with three swift, heavy stabs" (p. 379), in
what Lawrence intends as the efficacious blood sacrifice of traitors.
The conduct of the disorderly mob at the bullfight is contrasted with
that of Huitzilopochtli's men at the execution. The bullfight mob
screams and jostles and throws orange and banana peels and hats
(pp. 4–5). Outside, "two men stood making water against the wall, in
the interval of their excitement" (p. 15). Sterility as a product of imbalance on the side of white consciousness is suggested by Kate's
opinion that "these precious toreadors" look "like eunuchs, or women

in tight pants" (p. 8) and by the image of the horse "with its hind-quarters hitched up and the horn of the bull goring slowly and rhythmically in its vitals" (p. 14). This image, which presents the implied perversion of the matadors and the mob as really a kind of sado-masochistic sodomy, is paralleled, in the description of the attack on Jamiltepec, in the attitude of one of the bandits at death:

The bandit dropped on his knees again, and remained for a moment kneeling as if in prayer, the red pommel of the knife sticking out of his abdomen, from his white trousers. Then he slowly bowed over, doubled up, and went on his face again, once more with his buttocks in the air. [p. 293]

Ramón, in contrast to the bull in the parallel scene, simply lifts the man's chin and swiftly drives the knife into his throat (p. 294). Significantly, after both sacrificial rituals, rain falls. But after the heated excitement of the bullfight the rain is icy (p. 14), whereas after Ramón's cool defense of Jamiltepec the blood is washed "down into the cistern" so that "there will be blood in the water" they drink (p. 299).

Prurience is contrasted with instinctual innocence in responses to nakedness throughout the novel. The "full-fleshed, deep chested, rich body" of Ramón, with its "soft, cream-brown skin" and its "smooth, *pure* sensuality," makes Kate "shudder" and "feel dizzy." Kate, like Salome looking at John, cannot resist the "violation" of looking "with prying eyes" as she imagines "a knife stuck between those pure, male shoulders." Ramón is really "like a pomegranate on a dark tree in the distance, naked, but not undressed!" Kate recognizes that it is "better to lapse away from one's own prying assertive self, into the soft, untrespassing self, to whom nakedness is neither shame nor excitement, but clothed like a flower in its own deep, soft consciousness, beyond cheap awareness." "The itching, prurient, *knowing*, imagining eye" is the "curse of Eve," who in her fall was progenitor of the white consciousness. A return to the dark consciousness, then, is a return to a prelapsarian state of animal grace. "Ah!" Kate says to herself. "Let me close my eyes to him, and open only my soul." Carlota, in contrast, unable to bear the prurient itch of her own response to her husband's nakedness, asks him to "put something on" (pp. 179–182). Throughout the novel Indian women, unlike white women, observe nakedness without a flicker of prurience. The evolution of Kate's consciousness from white to dark is signaled by the change in her response to nakedness. When she marries Cipriano, both he and Ramón are stripped to

the waist (p. 326). Responsibility for maintaining instinctual innocence rests alike with viewer and object. The "chief toreador, . . .
lying on his bed all dressed up, smoking a fat cigar," seems to Villiers
"rather like a male Venus who is never undressed" (p. 21). The ex-
hibitionism of one and the prurience of the other are evident. Ramón,
in contrast to the toreador, strips to the waist to kill the bandits (p.
290), and Cipriano and the members of his guard strip to the waist to
execute the traitors (p. 370), thus differentiating between blood lust
and blood sacrifice. Nakedness in instinctual innocence becomes, in
fact, a basic symbol in Lawrence's equation of the prelapsarian and
pre-Columbian worlds. Occurring first in the nude stranger's emerging
from the lake to announce the return of the ancient gods (p. 51),
then in the nude man's rising beside Kate's boat to ask her tribute to
Quetzalcoatl (pp. 86–87), the symbol is repeated on the occasion of
any formal ritual in the Aztec revival.

3

The inverse parallel that Lawrence draws between Christian and
Aztec forms in contrasting white and dark consciousness recalls the
inversions of Christian forms in the Witches' Sabbath or Black Mass.
As George Lyman Kittredge describes the practice, "The rites are in
elaborate profanation of Christian ceremonies, which they reverse or
parody or burlesque."[8] The motif is thematically functional in Kate's
Bildungsroman, for, as Jules Michelet observes, "the *Black Mass,* in
its primary aspect," purposes the "redemption of Eve from the curse
Christianity had laid upon her."[9] Rather than limiting the ritual to a
formal inversion of the Mass, Lawrence parodies Christian Scripture
and tradition in a total mythic construct that becomes a basic symbol
in the opposition between light and dark. If in the process he does
violence to Christian concepts, he distorts just as greatly, when it suits
his purpose, the traditions of the historical Nahuatl religion of pre-
Columbian Mexico.

Following his customary practice Lawrence employs the Christian
tradition that pagan gods are manifestations of the devil. Satanic
colors of red and black and Satanic imagery of fire and serpent, drawn
from Aztec mythology, saturate the rituals of the revived ancient gods
as symbols of their dark opposition to the power of light emanating
from Christianity. To these images Lawrence adds statements which
are both too commonplace and too direct to be called symbolic. The
boatman who rows Kate down the lake has a "peculiar devilish half-
smile lurking under his face" (p. 102). Kate thinks of the Indians,

"They're like demons" (p. 105). Ramón says of himself, "Give the devil his dues" (p. 164). Cipriano remarks, "My manhood is like a devil inside me," and Ramón, whose own manhood "is like a demon howling inside," rages against its repression "like the devil" (p. 189). Cipriano's face is "the face at once of a god and a devil, the undying Pan face." Kate, recognizing in him the same pagan divinity that Lou found in St. Mawr, calls him "my demon lover!" (pp. 308–309). After their wedding one of the women boils water into which she flings white powder and yellow-brown flowers "as if she were a witch brewing decoctions" (p. 321).

Lawrence's consistent inversion of the Christian pattern begins with mythic statements on the subjects of creation, birth, and rebirth. In Christian tradition, "in the beginning was the Word, and the Word was with God, and the Word was God" (John 1:1). After reading reports of the ancient gods' return, Kate says to Ramón, "I love the *word* Quetzalcoatl," and he replies meaningfully, "The *word!*" (p. 56). Lawrence, like the Biblical writers, employs the mythic concept that Joseph Campbell calls "creation from the word, through naming the name."[10] But whereas Peter said to Jesus, "Thou hast the words of eternal life" (John 6:68), Ramón says, "The roots and the life are there. What else it needs is the word, for the forest to begin to rise again. And some man among men must speak the word" (p. 76). Angels at Christ's birth descended from the sky to tell the shepherds, "Fear not: . . . For unto you is born this day, in the city of David, a Saviour, which is Christ the Lord" (Luke 2:10–11); but at Quetzalcoatl's rebirth "a man of great stature" rises naked from the lake and says to the alarmed washerwomen on shore, "Why are you crying? Be quiet! . . . Your gods are ready to return to you" (p. 51). Christ was born of a Virgin (Luke 1:26–35), and so, according to Mme. Séjourné, were Quetzalcoatl and Huitzilopochtli:

In the Annals of Cuauhtitlan we read: ". . . it is said that the mother of Quetzalcoatl conceived because she swallowed an emerald stone." Huitzilopochtli's mother found herself pregnant after having in her bosom a white feather she had found while sweeping the temple. It would therefore seem that, as in the Christian mystery of the Incarnation, the spirit falls from on high to penetrate the body of a woman.[11]

However that may be, it suits Lawrence's purpose for the gods to be reborn as a result, not of parthenogenesis, but of a phallic miracle, from the lake of "frail-rippling, sperm-like water" (p. 89).

Both religions emphasize rebirth. In Christ's words, "Except a man be born again, he cannot see the kingdom of God" (John 3:3). Kate believes, "Ye must be born again. Even the gods must be born again" (p. 54). Christ promised, "I will come again and receive you unto myself" (John 14:3), and Lawrence arranges for Ramón to fulfill the Aztec prophecy of Quetzalcoatl's return.[12] Ramón tells Kate, "Ah, it is time now for Jesus to go back to the place of the death of the gods, and take the long bath of being made young again" (p. 57). In the Christian tradition the pagan gods, at Christ's coming, were dispelled, whereas in *The Plumed Serpent* it is Christ and the Virgin Mary who, at the return of Quetzalcoatl and Huitzilopochtli, are dispelled. The Christian tradition is seen, for example, in Milton's "On the Morning of Christ's Nativity":

> . . . from this happy day
> Th' old Dragon underground,
> In straiter limits bound,
> Not half so far casts his usurped sway . . .
> [ll. 167–170]

In the first hymn of Quetzalcoatl, conversely, Christ is quoted as saying:

> *My name is Jesus, I am Mary's Son.*
> *I am coming home.*
> *My mother, the moon is dark.*
> *Oh brother, Quetzalcoatl*
> *Hold back the dragon of the sun,*
> *Bind him with shadow while I pass*
> *Homewards. Let me come home.* [p. 115]

In the second hymn of Quetzalcoatl, Christ laments:

"The images stand in their churches, Oh Quetzalcoatl, they don't know that I and my Mother have departed. They are angry souls, Brother, my Lord! They vent their anger. They broke my Churches, they stole my strength, they withered the lips of the Virgin. They drove us away, and we crept away like a tottering old man and a woman, tearless and bent double with age. So we fled while they were not looking. And we seek but rest, to forget for ever the children of men who have swallowed the stone of despair." [pp. 224–225]

But "turbulent fellows" burlesque the mythic idea of the death and resurrection of the gods by invading one of the churches and throwing out the Christian images, hanging in their place the "gaudily-varnished dolls of papier-mâché" representing Judas which Mexicans explode during Easter week. Ramón expresses his regrets to the Bishop (pp. 258–262), and in a ceremony described as "reverent" he removes the tawdry Christian images from the Church of Sayula (pp. 279–280), burns them by the lake (p. 283), and subsequently reopens the church with images of Quetzalcoatl and Huitzilopochtli (p. 336).

Prayer in both religions is best offered in private. Jesus taught, ". . . when thou prayest, enter into thy closet, and, when thou hast shut thy door, pray to thy Father which is in secret" (Matthew 6:6), and Ramón's habit is to go to his room and close the windows and shutters, making it quite dark. But there the similarity ends. The Christian prayer is the Lord's Prayer (Matthew 6:9–13), and Christians customarily kneel. But Lawrence describes Ramón's prayer as follows:

He took off his clothes, and in the darkness thrust his clenched fists upwards above his head, in a terrible tension of stretched, upright prayer. In his eyes was only darkness, and slowly the darkness revolved in his brain, too, till he was mindless. Only a powerful will stretched itself and quivered from his spine in an immense tension of prayer. Stretched the invisible bow of the body in the darkness with inhuman tension, erect, till the arrows of the soul, mindless, shot to the mark, and the prayer reached its goal. [p. 166]

The word "will" is instructive not only because it counters the Christian's "Thy will be done" but also because, in the sexually connotative context of the passage, it evokes, contrary to Lawrence's intention, an image of that Laurentian anathema psychic masturbation. Mme. Séjourné says that "prayer and penitence formed the very nucleus of Quetzalcoatl's teaching,"[13] but far from being penitential, Ramón's is a "proud prayer" which he more and more ritualizes as physical gesture:

Then suddenly, in a concentration of intense, proud prayer, he flung his right arm up above his head, and stood transfixed, his left arm hanging softly by his side, the fingers touching his thigh. And on his face that fixed, intense look of pride which was at once a prayer. [p. 169]

Whereas Christians pray, "Give us this day our daily bread: . . . And lead us not into temptation, but deliver us from evil" (Matthew 6:11–13), Kate prays, "*Give me the mystery and let the world live again for me! . . . And deliver me from man's automatism*" (p. 101).

Carlota, who believes that Ramón's pride places him in mortal sin (p. 186), crawls down the aisle of the Church of Sayula at its reopening as the Church of Quetzalcoatl, crying hysterically:

"Lord! Lord Jesus! Make an end. Make an end, Lord of the world, Christ of the cross, make an end. Have mercy on him, Father. Have pity on him!
  "Oh, take his life from him now, now, that his soul may not die." [p. 340]

Kate, on the other hand, prays over the unconscious Ramón after the attack on Jamiltepec: "Oh, God! give the man his soul back, into this bloody body. Let the soul come back, or the universe will be cold for me and for many men" (p. 297). Christianity, as Lawrence presents it, affirms death of body and life of soul, whereas the Aztec revival affirms life of body and soul together.

Grace, in the Christian view, abounds as an effect of Christ's obedience to God in reversal of Adam's disobedience: "That as sin hath reigned unto death, even so might grace reign through righteousness unto eternal life by Jesus Christ our Lord" (Romans 5:21). But Kate's grace comes from sharing a communion of oranges and sandwiches with her Indian boatman: "*We are living! I know your sex, and you know mine. The mystery we are glad not to meddle with. You leave me my natural honour, and I thank you for the grace.*" The "pathos of grace" is "not of the spirit" but of the "dark, strong, unbroken blood, the flowering of the soul" (p. 103). It comes, furthermore, not from one's personal righteousness but from one's paradoxically proud submission to the dark gods. Ramón is optimistic about the outlook for Mexican regeneration because "these people don't assert any righteousness of their own. . . . That makes me think that grace is still with them" (p. 207).

Allusions to scriptural verbal structures reinforce the contrast between Christianity and the Aztec revival. Christ, who is called the "Prince of Peace," in the Sermon on the Mount said: "Blessed are the meek: for they shall inherit the earth" (Matthew 5:5), and "Blessed are the peacemakers: for they shall be called the children of God" (Matthew 5:9). In Ramón's view,

"The meek have inherited the earth, according to prophecy. But who am I, that I should envy them their peace? . . . Do I look like a gospel of peace?—or a gospel of war either? Life doesn't split down that division for me." [pp. 184–185]

Christ, at his last supper, "took bread, and gave thanks, and brake it, and gave unto [his disciples], saying, This is my body which is given for you: this do in remembrance of me" (Luke 22:19). When Kate rejects the "dingy-looking tortilla" that Concha thrusts at her, the girl laughs stridently, "Don't you want it? Don't you eat it?" and thinks, "She was one of those who won't eat bread: say they don't like it, that it is not food" (p. 210). In Lawrence's ironic ambiguity, Kate is rejecting the Eucharist of the dark gods. Whereas Jesus told Simon and Andrew, "Come ye after me, and I will make you to become fishers of men" (Mark 1:17), Ramón tells his followers, "We will be masters among men, and lords among men. But lords of men, and masters of men we will not be" (p. 175). Jesus promised for the faithful a heavenly reward in the afterlife (John 15:3), but Ramón, in his first sermon, insists, "There is no Before and After, there is only Now" (p. 172). Carlota places Christian emphasis on the virtue of charity (1 Corinthians 13:1–13), but Ramón tells her that the "white Anti-Christ of Charity, and socialism, and politics, and reform, will only succeed in finally destroying" Mexico (p. 206). Christ, tempted by the promise of power over "all the kingdoms of the world" in return for worshipping Satan, replied: "Get thee behind me, Satan: for it is written, Thou shalt worship the Lord thy God, and him only shalt thou serve" (Luke 4:5–8). Similarly, Ramón says, "I don't want to acquire a political smell. . . . It is not myself. It is the new spirit" (p. 243). Jesus had "the disciple . . . whom he loved" (John 19:26), and Ramón has Martin, his *mozo*, "the man who loved him" (p. 190).

Dark versions of the Christian sacraments of baptism, holy orders, matrimony, and the Eucharist initiate the questing soul into the faith of the dark gods. Christian baptism was instituted for the remission of sins and spiritual rebirth: "Therefore we are buried with him by baptism into death; that like as Christ was raised up from the dead by the glory of the Father, even so we also should walk in newness of life" (Romans 6:4). According to Mme. Séjourné, the Aztecs also had a sacrament of baptism for the remission of sins, thus revealing "an unsuspected level of inner development: purification and humility being the fundamentals of any true religious life."[14] In *The Plumed Serpent* the sacrament is parodied as Ramón and Cipriano swim together in the Lake of Sayula (p. 367), as Cipriano orders his men to "strip and wash" (p. 364), and as Kate, on her arrival at the lake, takes her ritual bath in the sperm-like water (p. 93). Lawrence uses the rite as a sacrament of rebirth into the Laurentian value of blood consciousness. There is, in the Christian Ordinal, a form for the making, ordination, and consecration of bishops, priests, and deacons, but none, it must be admitted, for the making of God Himself! Lawrence's parody of holy orders, therefore, is unique in its deification of Cipriano. In the form for the ordering of priests, the person to be ordained is examined by the bishop in formal dialogue, the Holy Spirit is invoked in litany to impart the sevenfold gifts of grace, and the ordination is completed by the bishop's laying hands on the receiver's head. In the creation of "the living Huitzilopochtli," Cipriano is examined by Ramón in formal dialogue and the sixfold gifts of darkness are invoked by Ramón's successively pressing manually, then binding with strips of black fur, the six mystical centers of Cipriano's body: eyes, heart, navel, loins, knees, and ankles. The Christian priest consciously accepts the authority and responsibility of his office but Cipriano falls into a state of "perfect unconsciousness," a sleep in which he puts on the mythic identity of the ancient god (pp. 365–367). Kate's and Cipriano's "marriage by Quetzalcoatl," similarly, parodies the Christian solemnization of matrimony, as formalized in *The Book of Common Prayer*. The Christian minister begins, "Dearly beloved, we are gathered together here in the sight of God, and in the face of this company, to join together this Man and this Woman in holy Matrimony. . . ." But Ramón says, "Barefoot on the living earth, with faces to the living rain, . . . at twilight, between the night and day; man, and woman, in presence of the unfading star, meet to be perfect in one another." Their marriage vows, likewise, parody traditional Christian vows. Kate repeats after Ramón, "I, a woman, beneath the darkness of this covering hand, pray to this man to meet me in the heart of the night, and never deny me. . . . But let it be an abiding place between us, for ever"; and Cipriano, with appropriate changes, says the same. The shift in form from vow to prayer signals the shift in emphasis from marital bond to marital relationship. Similarly, instead of the Christian minister's proclamation, "Those whom God hath joined together let no man put asunder," Ramón says, "Man shall betray a woman, and woman shall betray a man, . . . and it shall be forgiven them, each of them. But . . . . if either betray the abiding place of the two, it shall not be forgiven, neither by day nor by night nor in the twilight of the star" (pp. 326–327). Thus, Lawrence's focus is wholly on the sacramental union, not the civil contract, of marriage.

The order of worship in the religion of Quetzalcoatl, like the Witches' Sabbath, is a reverse parody of the Mass. The Introit opens with a Kyrie, *"Oye! Oye! Oye! Oye!"* followed by a Gloria, indicating that Ramón has forgotten all about his earlier goal to be a "lord among men," not a "lord of men":

> "Mary and Jesus have left you and gone to the place of renewal.
> And Quetzalcoatl has come. He is here.
> He is your lord." [p. 335]

The Litany is parodied in the repetition by the guard of Quetzalcoatl of nearly everything Ramón says and the Collect in the upright prayer, which has evolved by now into an extended arm salute. There is a sermon by Ramón as "the living Quetzalcoatl," followed by the Offertory: "A man shall take the wine of his spirit and the blood of his heart, the oil of his belly and the seed of his loins and offer them first to the Morning Star" (p. 339). These four essences represent, rather directly, the four dynamic centers of Lawrence's theory of psychic anatomy. Despite his protestation in *Fantasia of the Unconscious* that he deduces his "pollyanalytics" from his novels and poems, which "come unwatched out of one's pen" (p. 57), he is here attempting to deduce a novelistic element from the theory, which has now hardened into an object of mind. To put it another way, he is attempting the very "idealism" he condemns in *Psychoanalysis and the Unconscious* as "the motivizing of the great affective sources by means of ideas mentally derived" (p. 11). Ramón, as celebrant, mixes the yellow, red, black, and white liquids symbolizing the four essences. Then,

> he turned his back to the people and lifted the bowl high up between his hands, as if offering it to the image.
> Then suddenly he threw the contents of the bowl into the altar fire. [p. 339]

There is a concluding prayer, another salute, a Last Gospel, "The Omnipotent . . . is with me, and I serve Omnipotence!" and a concluding hymn (pp. 334–342).

Traditionally the Witches' Sabbath includes the defloration of a virgin. According to Michelet, "the woman . . . was at once altar and sacrifice."[15] In *The Plumed Serpent* this element is reserved for a later chapter. After Cipriano, who seems to Kate "to be driving the male significance to its utmost, and beyond, with a sort of demonism" (pp. 384–385), has executed the traitors, he takes Kate to the church, where, before the black idol, he "held her hand in silence, till she was

Malintzi, and virgin for him," and their "two flames rippled in one-ness" (p. 392). Lawrence's parody of Benjamin Franklin's list of virtues provides a useful gloss on this scene. Under "Chastity" Lawrence wrote, "Only know that 'venery' is of the great gods. An offering-up of yourself to the very great gods, the dark ones, and nothing else." But the "venery" in front of the stone idol, in its complete reification of the earlier spontaneous insight, violates Lawrence's own injunction against using sex for motives other than one's "passional impulse."

Eliseo Vivas ably supports his view that Lawrence's preconceptions about the relationship between the common people and the Roman Catholic Church in Mexico blinded him to the reality of the situation.[16] But one really needs no such evidence to find the interview between Ramón and the Bishop, which Father William Tiverton thinks is "the dramatic centre of the novel,"[17] plainly incredible. Ramón is clearly intended to affirm the mythic unity of all gods, but his remark that "Catholic Church means the Church of All, the Universal Church" seems, in context, fatuous. The Bishop is supposed to be a prelate of considerable stature, but his reply to Ramón, "I do not understand these clever things you are saying to me," unless he is being cruelly facetious, is scarcely literate. The one believable exchange between the two follows Ramón's announcement that he intends to expropriate the Church of Sayula. The Bishop reminds him that "it is illegal," and Ramón, who has already intimidated the Bishop with Cipriano's presence as General Viedma, replies with a threat: "What is illegal in Mexico? . . . What is weak is illegal. I will not be weak" (pp. 261–263).

It is not the dark gods, of course, but Cipriano's army that conquers Mexico. If the dark sun, the circle dance, the plumed serpent, and some of the hymns are artistically effective, the ersatz rituals often seem less vital and primitive than vulgar and bombastic. And when pseudo-religious bombast is used as political propaganda in support of a war machine, it is hardly surprising that people respond as puppets of the state rather than as free individuals in such instances of mass hypnosis as Ramón's parody of the Mass:

In three successive instants the faces of the men inside the chancel were lit bluish, then gold, then dusky red. And in the same moment Ramón had turned to the people and shot up his hand.

"Salute Quetzalcoatl!" cried a voice, and men began to thrust up their arms. . . . [p. 339]

Mme. Séjourné, who says that Quetzalcoatl was originally a Nahuatl god of an older spiritual order, comments, pertinently enough, on the perversion and betrayal of his spiritual legacy in the power politics of the Aztec empire:

To take their religious explanations of war seriously is to fall into a trap of State propaganda. . . . The Aztec nobles were never themselves impatient to achieve the Solar glory in whose name they were slaughtering humanity. . . . In fact, everything points to the conclusion that the Aztec lords, although brought up in the doctrine of Quetzalcoatl, which taught men that inner perfection and spiritual sacrifice were supreme goals, had come to think of ritual slaughter only as a political necessity.[18]

Cipriano, Ramón's hatchet-man, is about as scrupulous as his Aztec prototypes:

He stripped his captives and tied them up. But if it seemed a brave man, he would swear him in. If it seemed to him a knave, a treacherous cur, he stabbed him to the heart, saying:
"I am the red Huitzilopochtli, of the knife." [p. 364]

The guards' automatism leaves them unmoved by the dazzling inconsistency by which Cipriano rationalizes his murder of the prisoners:

Cipriano: "When many men come against one, what is the name of the many?"
Guards: "Cowards, my Lord."
Cipriano: "Cowards it is. They are less than men. Men that are less than men are not good enough for the light of the sun. If men that are men will live, men that are less than men must be put away, lest they multiply too much. Men that are more than men have the judgment of men that are less than men. Shall they die?"
Guards: "They shall surely die, my Lord." [p. 377]

Obsessed with the question, Kate wonders, "Why should I judge him? He is of the gods. . . . What do I care if he kills people?" (p. 392). But her protestations establish only her own ambivalence, a realistic reflection in her character of the fatal division which besets the Aztec movement. For in a gradual shift in emphasis, inward concerns are replaced by outward concerns, religious experience by power politics and military conquest:

Then a kind of war began. The Knights of Cortés brought out their famous hidden store of arms, . . . and a clerical mob headed by a fanatical priest surged into the Zócalo. Montes had the guns turned on them. . . . In the churches, the priests were still inflaming the orthodox to a holy war. In the streets, priests who had gone over to Quetzalcoatl were haranguing the crowd.

It was a wild moment. In Zacatecas General Narciso Beltran had declared against Montes and for the Church. But Cipriano with his Huitzilopochtli soldiers had attacked with such swiftness and ferocity, Beltran was taken and shot, his army disappeared.

Then Montes declared the old Church illegal in Mexico, and caused a law to be passed, making the religion of Quetzalcoatl the national religion of the Republic. All churches were closed. All priests were compelled to take an oath of allegiance to the Republic, or condemned to exile. The armies of Huitzilopochtli and the white and blue *serapes* of Quetzalcoatl appeared in all the towns and villages of the Republic. . . . [pp. 418–419]

The religious revival, in other words, follows the all too familiar pattern of the military coup d'etat.

4

When a symbolic structure is so carefully founded as that of *The Plumed Serpent,* it is difficult to see how the work could go so wrong in novelistic detail. Both the theme and the symbols by which it is concretized are worthy of serious critical consideration. A reconciliation of the opposites of white consciousness and dark consciousness can be effected, Lawrence implies, only through creative being in "the dreamless Now" (p. 173). The nature of this existence is stated metaphorically in various symbols of unity. If Quetzalcoatl is a god, he must be "Lord of the Two Ways" (p. 253). Mme. Séjourné confirms that "the spiritual message of Quetzalcoatl deals with the resolution of the painful problem of human duality,"[19] that is, of the conflict between flesh and spirit. Ramón, accordingly, must invoke both the snake of the earth and the bird of the air (p. 195). Hence, in his proud, upright prayer, the right hand is upraised to receive the bird of the spirit and the left hand hangs at the side to receive the snake of the flesh. Hence, also, the Eye of Quetzalcoatl, the plumed serpent, joins the attributes of bird and snake.

Reconciliation between flesh and spirit results in the achievement of centrality. If Kate sees "in the eyes of so many white people, the look of nullity," she also notices that "the strange, soft flame of courage in the black Mexican eyes . . . was not knit to a centre, that centre which is the soul of a man in a man" (pp. 73–74). Man, as Kate discovers, is "not created ready-made": "Men and women had incomplete selves, made up of bits assembled together loosely and somewhat haphazard" (p. 102). Through ritual, Ramón hopes to unify the pieces, to aid man in his self-creation. He advises, "And let your navel know nothing of yesterday, and go into your women with a new body, enter the new body in her" (p. 197). The sexual union of male and female, in the polar equilibrium of the Morning Star and the Evening Star shining together, is sacramental (p. 338).

The concept of centrality is expressed appropriately in circle imagery. If the circle itself can be called a Jungian mandala symbol, the archetype whereby the self seeks to unify the various components of the personality,[20] Lawrence places within this magic circle a divine center, the mythic construct of the World Navel. Mircea Eliade formulates the architectonic symbolism of the Center as follows:

1. The Sacred Mountain—where heaven and earth meet—is situated at the center of the world.
2. Every temple or palace—and, by extension, every sacred city or royal residence—is a Sacred Mountain, thus becoming a Center.
3. Being an *axis mundi,* the sacred city or temple is regarded as the meeting point of heaven, earth, and hell.[21]

Furthermore, since "every creation repeats the pre-eminent cosmogonic act, the Creation of the world," "whatever is founded has its foundation at the center of the world."[22] Thus, in *The Plumed Serpent,* the achievement of centrality—in the eyes, in the navel, in the circle dance, in the dark sun, in the self—is, mythically, the repetition of divine creation, the achievement of godhead through creation of the self.

The brilliance of Lawrence's symbolic conception notwithstanding, most critics perceive a failure in coherence between the realistic and metaphorical modes of the novel. F. R. Leavis finds the evocation of the "pagan renascence" "willed and mechanical" or, at the least, "monotonous and boring."[23] Graham Hough says that Lawrence abandons the method of the novelist for that of the "amateur mystagogue, and the result is the windy emptiness of the Quetzalcoatl hymns and the dressed-up absurdity of what the protagonists know to be a kind of charade." The moral disintegration which follows closely upon this formal disintegration is marked by "violent intrusions . . . of sexual anger, quasi-Fascist deifications of discipline and a relish for cruelty."[24] H. M. Daleski, recalling Lawrence's charge that Tolstoy applied the world to a metaphysic which he had constructed for his own self-justification, observes that if Lawrence's effort to reconcile the male and female sides of his consciousness resulted in a body of work unrivaled in its organic development, "his attempt, in *The Plumed Serpent*, to assert a 'male' metaphysic in order 'to justify himself' is disastrous."[25] E. W. Tedlock, Jr., finding "the formal religious development . . . embarrassingly pseudo-poetic, preachy, and posturing," points out that the emphasis on "punishment, execution, war, and state sanction suggests a theocratic intolerance potentially as anti-life as the status quo Lawrence opposed."[26] R. P. Draper suggests that since Kate and Cipriano have only a sexual, not a personal, relationship, they really have "no marriage at all." Her acceptance of him as a poetic symbol is "beautifully created," but "he is incredible as an actual partner for whose sake Kate is willing to abandon all her old notions of freedom and independence."[27] Julian Moynahan thinks that the novel directly translates Lawrence's recommendation in *Fantasia of the Unconscious* that the ruling classes govern "by controlling and dictating the symbols to which [the] ignorant masses give unconscious and inevitable obedience." Ramón and Cipriano maintain power in their "semi-priestly, semi-military dictatorship" "by waving the symbols of the Quetzalcoatl cult before the dazed eyes of the Mexican masses."[28] Eliseo Vivas condemns Lawrence's program on the grounds that he presents a counterfeit religion rather than the actual "blood-madness" of the Aztecs; that his desire "to give back *life* to the Mexicans," even if realized, would not solve "all other problems that confront modern man"; that Ramón as saviour, far from concerning himself with his people's welfare, does not act from the usual motives of reformers and revolutionists; and that Lawrence's idea of the inadequacy of Jesus and the Roman Catholic Church for Mexico does not correspond to reality.[29] Mark Spilka asserts that although Quetzalcoatl is supposed to be the lord of two ways—"blood and spirit, earth and sky, dark and daylight"—the second way of "the mental-spiritual consciousness . . . remains singularly 'unfused' in the course of the novel. . . ."[30] Harry T. Moore considers *The Plumed Serpent*, as a travel book, unsurpassed in its evocation of the Mexican scene but objects to the philosophy in the book: "Myth and symbol are one thing; we have learned, in our time, that to have them incarnated in a government which will coerce those who don't submit to its myth and symbol, to its mass hypnosis, is quite another." His evaluation of the work as "at once Lawrence's most ambitious attempt in the area of the novel and his most notable failure"[31] summarizes the consensus of all but a few.

The few exceptions, however, are noteworthy. William York Tindall, who made the first study of Lawrence's sources in the archaeology of Mrs. Zelia Nuttall and the theosophy of Mme. H. P. Blavatsky, calls *The Plumed Serpent* "by far his best novel as well as the outstanding example of primitivism in our time."[32] Jascha Kessler, attempting to salvage the real story from "the clumsy superstructure of the novel's manifest content" by means of explicating the monomythic pattern, asserts that "everything in *The Plumed Serpent*, all the politics and religious demagoguery, seems irrelevant when we compare it with the drama of the hidden primal mythic adventure it subserves."[33] John B. Vickery also defends the view that reducing the novel to a program is an injustice to Lawrence. Ramón's quest, symbolic rather than ideological, is not so much for "a revival of pre-Columbian religion" as for "the attainment of an integrated personality." As "complementary figures," Ramón and Kate follow respectively "the way of action" and "the way of comprehension, of the critical intelligence that follows upon the act and attempts to understand it." The novel ends irresolutely where Kate is concerned not because the two ways to integration are irreconcilable, but because Ramón wisely resists the temptation to make the decision which must be ultimately Kate's responsibility.[34] L. D. Clark, in *Dark Night of the Body: D. H. Lawrence's "The Plumed Serpent,"* after admitting its flaws, presents the fullest defense of the novel yet mounted:

The worst side of Lawrence was never more evident than it is in this novel: the careless language, the wearisome repetitions, the prophetic aspirations, the confusion of practical with artistic ends. But two things save the book from the author: Lawrence's profound sympathy with the land he was writing about, and his uncanny skill at synthesizing form and setting and symbol.[35]

In succeeding chapters Clark examines in scholarly detail Lawrence's relation to the American continent, Kate's quest for the way from disillusionment to fulfillment, the ceremonial content of the Quetzalcoatl revival, the sources in pre-Columbian mythology, and the symbolism of the circle. Such studies as these four argue persuasively for acceptance of Lawrence's thematic intention for his formal accomplishment. But a more compelling consideration is the inseparability of theme and form.

What went wrong in the novel, for all Lawrence's carefully founded symbolic structure, was, finally, unity, the coherence of components in that artistic integrity lacking which any work of art, whatever the quality of its parts, is doomed to a measure of failure. In *The Plumed Serpent* the contradiction between positive and negative values makes impossible the realization of the central theme, the reconciliation of opposites through creative being. The positive values of the novel are those of Lawrence's dynamic metaphysic: the vitality of growth in Kate's oscillating response to the Aztec revival; the organic imperfection of the ending, typically Laurentian in its tentativeness, its irresolution of Kate's dilemma about staying in Mexico; the creative imagination behind the moral and psychic energy of such cosmic symbols of unity as the dark sun, the circle dance, the plumed serpent. But operating against Lawrence's romanticism are the negative values of the novel, those of the static metaphysic: the mechanism of the supposedly spontaneous but actually carefully manipulated revival; the uniformitarian system which derives, inevitably, from the unholy alliance of theological, political, and military power; the conscious, if not entirely rational, progressive reification of symbols, originally cosmic in their conception, into mere objects of will.

Horace Gregory remarks on Kate's indecision, "The half gods of Mexico cannot bring to full birth the conversion of a single white woman."[36] After their marriage by Ramón, Cipriano says to Kate pathetically: "I *am* the living Huitzilopochtli . . . I *am* he.—Am I not?" (p. 320). But anyone who needs reassurance that he is a god, isn't! Kate, significantly, marries Cipriano only in Quetzalcoatl; she balks every time the idea of a legal civil ceremony is mentioned. In the end she still vacillates between what has been really a dynamic love experience and her personal perception of the degree of staticism that, with Cipriano, accompanies it. She considers, small wonder, getting "back to simple life": "Without all this abstraction, and *will*. Life is good enough for me if I am allowed to live and be myself" (p. 439). It is a wise perception; and it reflects, on one level, Lawrence's own perception of what was wrong with *The Plumed Serpent*.

Three of Lawrence's letters about the novel are frequently cited. In a letter to Curtis Brown (23 June 1925), he calls *The Plumed Serpent* "my most important novel, so far." Just after leaving America he writes to Martin Secker ("Friday," probably 9 October 1925): "Tell the man, very nice man, in your office, I *do* mean what Ramón means—for all of us.—" Three years later, absorbed in *Lady Chatterley's Lover*, Lawrence, in a letter to Witter Bynner (13 March 1928), in effect rejects the political side of the earlier novel:

I sniffed the red herring in your last letter a long time: then at last decide it's a live sprat. I mean about *The Plumed Serpent* and the "hero." On the whole, I think you're right. The hero is obsolete, and the leader of men is a back number. After all, at the back of the hero is the militant ideal: and the militant ideal, or the ideal militant, seems to me also a cold egg. We're sort of sick of all forms of militarism and militantism, and *Miles* is a name no more, for a man. On the whole I agree with you, the leader-cum-follower relationship is a bore. And the new relationship will be some sort of tenderness, sensitive, between men and men and men and women, and not the one up one down, lead on I follow, *ich dien* sort of business.

Tenderness, as a genuine principle of love, is discernible in the relationships of the major characters in *The Plumed Serpent,* though amid all the swelled godheads, it is never really an end in itself but is exploited in the manipulation of the Aztec revival. But genuine feeling, in fiction as in life, rarely survives such exploitation. As Lawrence says in "Morality and the Novel":

If you try to nail anything down, in the novel, either it kills the novel, or the novel gets up and walks away with the nail.
Morality in the novel is the trembling instability of the balance. When the novelist puts his thumb in the scale, to pull down the balance to his own predilection, that is immorality. [*Phoenix,* p. 528]

And that, perhaps, is the major reason why the dualities of *The Plumed Serpent* remain unreconciled.

NOTES

1. "The Duality of Lawrence," *Modern Fiction Studies,* V (Spring, 1959), 5.

2. *D. H. Lawrence: A Basic Study of His Ideas* (Gainesville, Fla.: University of Florida Press, 1955), p. 181.

3. Graham Hough, *The Dark Sun: A Study of D. H. Lawrence* (New York: The Macmillan Co., 1957), p. 136.

4. Jascha Kessler, "Descent in Darkness: The Myth of *The Plumed Serpent,*" in *A D. H. Lawrence Miscellany,* ed. Harry T. Moore (Carbondale, Ill.: Southern Illinois University Press, 1959), p. 243.

5. William York Tindall, *D. H. Lawrence and Susan His Cow* (New York: Columbia University Press, 1939), pp. 113–117, 124–161.

6. Laurette Séjourné, *Burning Water: Thought and Religion in Ancient Mexico* (London and New York: Thames and Hudson, 1956), p. 28.

7. *Feeling and Form* (New York: Charles Scribner's Sons, 1953), pp. 196–197.

8. *Witchcraft in Old and New England* (New York: Russell & Russell, 1956), p. 243.

9. Jules Michelet, *Satanism and Witchcraft: A Study in Medieval Superstition,* trans. A. R. Allinson (New York: The Citadel Press, 1939), p. 102.

10. Joseph Campbell, *The Masks of God: Primitive Mythology* (New York: The Viking Press, 1959), p. 86.

11. Séjourné, p. 56.

12. Campbell, *The Masks of God: Primitive Mythology,* p. 460.

13. Séjourné, p. 27.

14. Séjourné, p. 9.

15. Michelet, p. 107.

16. Eliseo Vivas, *D. H. Lawrence: The Failure and the Triumph of Art* (London: George Allen and Unwin Ltd., 1961), pp. 73–84.

17. *D. H. Lawrence and Human Existence* (London: Rockliff, 1951), p. 71.

18. Séjourné, p. 35.

19. Ibid., p. 64.

20. See Calvin S. Hall and Gardner Lindzey, *Theories of Personality* (New York: John Wiley and Sons, Inc., 1957), pp. 83–85.

21. *Cosmos and History: The Myth of the Eternal Return,* trans. Willard R. Trask (New York: Harper and Brothers, 1959), p. 12.

22. Ibid., p. 18.

23. *D. H. Lawrence: Novelist* (New York: Alfred A. Knopf, 1956), p. 71.

24. Hough, pp. 129–138.

25. *The Forked Flame: A Study of D. H. Lawrence* (Evanston, Ill.: Northwestern University Press, 1965), pp. 251–252.

26. *D. H. Lawrence: Artist and Rebel: A Study of Lawrence's Fiction* (Albuquerque: University of New Mexico Press, 1963), p. 192.

27. *D. H. Lawrence* (New York: Twayne Publishers, Inc., 1964), pp. 108–109.

28. *The Deed of Life: The Novels and Tales of D. H. Lawrence* (Princeton: Princeton University Press, 1963), pp. 109–110.

29. Vivas, pp. 77–85.

30. *The Love Ethic of D. H. Lawrence* (Bloomington: Indiana University Press, Midland Book, 1957), p. 210.

31. *"The Plumed Serpent:* Vision and Language," in *D. H. Lawrence: A Collection of Critical Essays,* ed. Mark Spilka (Englewood Cliffs, N.J.: Prentice-Hall, Inc., 1963), pp. 61–69.

32. Tindall, p. 113.

33. Kessler, p. 258.

34. *"The Plumed Serpent* and the Eternal Paradox," *Criticism,* V (1963), 119–134.

35. (Austin: University of Texas Press, 1964), p. 13.

36. *D. H. Lawrence: Pilgrim of the Apocalypse: A Critical Study* (New York: Grove Press, Inc., Evergreen Books Edition, 1957), p. 73.

CHAPTER EIGHT

Toward the Greater Day

WHEN D. H. LAWRENCE left America on 22 September 1925, he was exhausted, both physically and spiritually, by the effort of finishing *The Plumed Serpent*, by the serious illness of the preceding winter, and by the fierce engagement of three years with the American continent and people. Nevertheless, some positive transformations were taking place in his life and thought, and these were reflected subsequently in his work.

LAWRENCE'S RESPONSE TO AMERICA

After completing the novel in February, 1925, Lawrence collapsed with what he described variously as 'flu, malaria, grippe, typhoid, or a combination of these; for although Dr. Uhlfelder in Mexico City had diagnosed the disease as tuberculosis, Lawrence would not use the word. The illness delayed for six months the departure originally planned for 10 March 1925.

With his weakened physical condition and with the natural letdown that followed upon the completion of such a major creative undertaking as *The Plumed Serpent*, Lawrence was, small wonder, living by this time on the frayed ends of his emotions. To make matters worse, letters from Dorothy Brett and John Middleton Murry forced him repeatedly to traverse the old ground of his last painful visit to England. He writes candidly to Miss Brett ("Monday morning," probably 26 January 1925):

We are creatures of two halves, spiritual and sensual—and each half is as important as the other. Any relation based on the one half—say the delicate spiritual half alone—*inevitably* brings revulsion and betrayal. It is halfness, or partness, which causes Judas.

124

Then, after discussing the "halfness" of Miss Brett's various friendships, which are characterized, he says, by spiritualized sensuality, "sex in the head," Lawrence adds: "No, Brett. I do not want your friendship, till you have a full relation somewhere, a *kindly* relation of both halves, not *in part*, as all your friendships have been." To Murry he writes sarcastically (28 January 1925):

You remember that charming dinner at the Café Royal that night? You remember saying: I love you, Lorenzo, but I won't promise not to betray you? Well, you *can't* betray me, and that's all there is to that. *Ergo*, just leave off loving me. Let's wipe off all that Judas-Jesus slime.

On the same day he writes to Miss Brett: "Don't send me any more Murry letters. The smell of that London stink I want no more in my nostrils." Struggling painfully to free himself of destructive personal entanglements, which at this point can only add emotional stress to his physical illness, Lawrence adds: "I am tired to death of all the indecencies of intimacies. I want to be left alone. There must be a complete new attitude. And till then, silence about all this stuff."

On his return to the ranch Lawrence recounts the whole sequence of his illness in a letter to Amy Lowell (6 April 1925):

I got malaria in Oaxaca: then grippe: then a typhoid inside: was so sick, I wearied of the day. Struggled to Mexico City, was put to bed again for three weeks—then packed off up here. We had booked our passages to England, but the doctor said I *must* stay in the sun, he wouldn't be answerable for me if I went on the sea, and to England. So we came here. The Emigration Authorities at El Paso treated us as Emigrants, and nearly killed me a second time: this after the Consul and the Embassy people in Mexico —the American—had been most kind, doing things to make it easier for us. They only made it harder. The Emigration Dept. is Dept. of Labour, and you taste the Bolshevist method in its conduct.

However—after two days' fight we got through—and yesterday got to our little ranch.

Lawrence is also aware of how much *The Plumed Serpent*, which had not yet acquired its translated title, had taken in will and feeling. As he writes to Miss Lowell:

I managed to finish my Mexican novel *Quetzalcoatl* in Mexico: the very day I went down, as if shot in the intestines. But I daren't even look at the outside of the MS. It cost one so much, and I wish I could eat all the lotus that ever budded, and drink up Lethe to the source. Talk about dull opiates— one wants something that'll go into the very soul.

Lawrence is ready, by this time, to leave America and to reintegrate the pieces of his European identity. As he writes to Mrs. G. R. G. Conway (2 April 1925): "I have a lurking hankering for Europe. I think at the end of the summer, we shall both sail." In a subsequent letter to Mrs. Conway (28 August 1925), he is still of the same mind: "But I feel I want to get out of America Loca for a while: I believe it sends *everybody* a bit loco." Yet he adds ambivalently: "It grieves me to leave my horses, and my cow Susan, and the cat Timsy Wemyss, and the white cock Moses—and the place. Next time you pass, call here at this ranch instead of at Hergesheimer's house: it's very wonderful country."

At the root of Lawrence's ambivalence lay his growing recognition that his sojourn in America had represented a sharply divided experience, an experience marked by his divergent responses, on the one hand, to the organicism of the American continent and, on the other, to the mechanism of the materialistic society which was exploiting it.

Aboriginal America embodied for Lawrence a religious experience of a kind radically different from that of traditional Christianity. In "New Mexico," an essay published in *Phoenix: The Posthumous Papers of D. H. Lawrence* (1936), his statement on the subject is unequivocal:

I think New Mexico was the greatest experience from the outside world that I have ever had. It certainly changed me for ever. Curious as it may sound, it was New Mexico that liberated me from the present era of civilization, the great era of material and mechanical development. Months spent in holy Kandy, in Ceylon, the holy of holies of southern Buddhism, had not touched the great psyche of materialism and idealism which dominated me. And years, even in the exquisite beauty of Sicily, right among the old Greek paganism that still lives there, had not shattered the essential Christianity on which my character was established. . . .

But the moment I saw the brilliant, proud morning shine high up over the deserts of Santa Fé, something stood still in my soul, and I started to attend. . . . In the magnificent fierce morning of New Mexico one sprang awake, a new part of the soul woke up suddenly, and the old world gave way to a new. [p. 142]

As L. D. Clark says, "It is no exaggeration to speak of Lawrence's deepest experience with the American continent as mystical."[1] For in New Mexico he experienced the divinity that permeates the natural and physical world. As he describes the religion of the Indians in "New Mexico":

It was a vast old religion, greater than anything we know: more starkly and nakedly religious. There is no God, no conception of a god. All is god. But it is not the pantheism we are accustomed to, which expresses itself as "God is everywhere, God is in everything." In the oldest religion, everything was alive, not supernaturally but naturally alive. . . . For the whole life-effort of man was to get his life into direct contact with the elemental life of the cosmos, mountain-life, cloud-life, thunder-life, air-life, earth-life, sun-life. To come into immediate *felt* contact, and so derive energy, power, and a dark sort of joy. This effort into sheer naked contact, without an *intermediary or mediator*, is the root meaning of religion. . . . [pp. 146–147]

But in white America's exploitation of the continent for materialistic ends Lawrence found the seeds of destruction of the regenerate society which had been its potential. White America's conversion of the Indian into a mere tourist attraction revealed its rejection of the genuinely religious truth embodied in the Indians' rituals. In a letter to Willard Johnson (probably 3 August 1924), Lawrence describes a Hopi snake dance:

Just a show! The Southwest is the great playground of the white American. The desert isn't good for anything else. But it does make a fine national playground. And the Indian, with his long hair and his bits of pottery and blankets and clumsy home-made trinkets, he's a wonderful live toy to play with. More fun than keeping rabbits and just as harmless.

And the Indians, thus exploited, take on the attributes of their exploiters. In a letter to John Middleton Murry (17 November 1924), Lawrence tells of meeting the governor of Oaxaca: "Fancy, even a Zapotec Indian, when he becomes governor, is only a fellow in a Sunday suit grinning and scheming."

American society's preference for surface sensation to inward experience, for utilitarian object to vitalistic truth, makes genuine creativity all but impossible in America. Thus, Lawrence writes to Kyle Crichton (31 August 1925) in response to the manuscript of a story the American writer had sent to him:

You don't concern yourself with the *human inside* at all, only with the insides of steel works. It's the sort of consciousness the working man has: but at the same time he's got a passionate sub-conscious. And it's this *sub-conscious* which makes the story: otherwise you have journalism.

As he elaborates in a subsequent letter to Crichton, written aboard the S. S. *Resolute* (28 September 1925):

I have [been] thinking of what you say about not having the courage to be a creative writer. It seems to me that may be true—America, of all countries, kills that courage, simply because it sees no value in the really creative effort, whereas it esteems, more highly than any other country, the journalistic effort: it loves a thrill or a sensation, but loathes to be in any way *moved,* inwardly affected so that a new vital adjustment is necessary. Americans are enormously adaptable: perhaps because inwardly they are not adjusted at all to their environment. They are never American as a chipmunk is, or as an Indian is: only as a Ford car or as the Woolworth building.
   That's why it seems to me impossible almost, to be purely a creative writer in America: everybody compromises with journalism and commerce.

The ego-assertiveness which makes integration in a truly creative society all but impossible is not, however, an exclusively American but a broadly human tendency. After his "Last Supper" at the Café Royal, Lawrence returned to New Mexico with only one disciple, and in her he perceived a fatal split between will and feeling, not the wholeness of the Holy Ghost. Yet finally he was honest enough to extend the same judgment to himself and to give up the metaphor of the creative society which he had once conceived as a literal possibility. In a letter to Dorothy Brett ("Saturday," Spring, 1925), he concludes that with most people, himself included, "the spirit, the flow, is always toward separating":

A life in common is an illusion, when the instinct is always to divide, to separate individuals and set them one against the other. And this seems to be the ruling instinct, unacknowledged. Unite with the one against the other. And it's no good.

To quote Harry T. Moore: *"Il n'y a pas de Rananim."*[2]

"THE FLYING FISH"

   "The Flying Fish," a brilliant but unfinished story begun in 1925 but not published until the *Phoenix* volume of 1936, has received scant attention from critics.[3] Yet this fragment, the first pages of which Lawrence dictated to Frieda when he was still too ill to write,[4] is significant for its reflection of Lawrence's attempt not only to reconcile metaphorically the ambivalent views with which he was emerging from his experience of the American continent and people but also to come to terms with the prospect of his own death, which he had realized in his illness.

Lying seriously ill of malaria in a South Mexican town, the British writer Gethin Day receives a cablegram from his sister Lydia: "Come home else no Day in Daybrook." In the allusion to his ancestor Sir Gilbert Day's *Book of Days:*

> No Day in Daybrook;
> For the Vale a bad outlook [p. 780],

he recognizes that his sister is dying. Never shown to outsiders and read but rarely in the family "at twilight, when the evening star shone," this "secret family bible" is counterpointed with the present narrative throughout the fragment as a mythic gloss on Gethin Day's experience. The *Book of Days* thematically centers in the contrasting concepts of the Greater Day and the lesser day:

"Beauteous is the day of the yellow sun which is the common day of men; but even as the winds roll unceasing above the trees of the world, so doth that Greater Day, which is the Uncommon Day, roll over the unclipt bushes of our little daytime. Even also as the morning sun shakes his yellow wings on the horizon and rises up, so the great bird beyond him spreads out his dark blue feathers, and beats his wings in the tremor of the Greater Day." [p. 782]

From the cablegram, Gethin Day realizes that his dying sister is emerging now into the world of the Greater Day. He realizes, moreover, from his Mexican experience and from his own desperate illness, what this means:

. . . in the last years, something in the hard, fierce, finite sun of Mexico, in the dry terrible land, and in the black staring eyes of the suspicious natives, had made the ordinary day lose its reality to him. It had cracked like some great bubble, and to his uneasiness and terror, he had seemed to see through the fissures the deeper blue of that other Greater Day where moved the other sun shaking its dark blue wings. Perhaps it was the malaria; perhaps it was his own inevitable development; perhaps it was the presence of those handsome, dangerous, wide-eyed men left over from the ages before the flood in Mexico, which caused his old connexions and his accustomed world to break for him. He was ill, and he felt as if at the very middle of him, beneath his navel, some membrane were torn, some membrane which had connected him with the world and its day. The natives who attended him, quiet, soft, heavy, and rather helpless, seemed, he realized, to be gazing from their wide black eyes always into that greater day whence they had come and where they wished to return. Men of a dying race, to whom the busy sphere of the common day is a cracked and leaking shell. [pp. 782–783]

With romanticists like Lawrence immortality is never a static concept, a changeless heaven of monolithic splendor. Permanence, rather, is to be found in the unremitting organic cycle of birth, life, and death. In the symbolic construct of the Greater Day, Lawrence catches, if only fragmentarily, the hidden portion of the cycle, the larger context of mythic time in which linear time is contained. Yet however valuable it may be for man to integrate in his consciousness an awareness of this larger context, mythic time is not finally appropriate as the single measure of temporal, mortal experience.

Whereas most modern civilized men live only in the lesser day of getting and spending, Gethin Day, Lawrence's last literary persona of the American period, has been lured too long by the siren call of the dark, the deep, the Greater Day. Having glimpsed in his desperate illness the ultimate dissolution of his individual consciousness, he must, in response to his sister's call, return to his ancestral home, Daybrook, to reintegrate the opposites of his psychic experience. He must, symbolically, delimit the waters of the "brook" of unconscious, mythic, primitive modes of awareness by drawing the circumference of the "day" of conscious, linear, traditional modes of western civilization. Thus, the message, "Come home else no Day in Daybrook," is a call to incarnate the timeless insights of the mythic perspective in the historical dimension of one's only life cycle. For only in balancing these opposing forces within the self can he, paradoxically, both achieve individual identity and prepare for its dissolution in death:

He wanted to go home. He didn't care now whether England was tight and little and over-crowded and far too full of furniture. He no longer minded the curious quiet atmosphere of Daybrook in which he had felt he would stifle as a young man. He no longer resented the weight of family tradition, nor the peculiar sense of authority which the house seemed to have over him. Now he was sick from the soul outwards, and the common day had cracked for him, and the uncommon day was showing him its immensity, he felt that home was the place. It did not matter that England was small and tight and over-furnished, if the Greater Day were round about. He wanted to go home, away from these big wild countries where men were dying back into the Greater Day, home where he dare face the sun behind the sun, and come into his own in the Greater Day. [p. 783]

Daybrook, moreover, is the appropriate place for Gethin Day to go in search of his own selfhood. Sir Gilbert, who had built the present ancestral mansion in the sixteenth century, had described it as a place, like Oedipus's triple crossroads, where three ways meet—the Sacred Center at the meeting point of birth, life, and death: " 'Daybrook standeth at the junction of the ways at the centre of the trefoil. Even it rides within the Vale as an ark between three seas; being indeed the ark of these vales, if not of all England' " (p. 781).

With a metaphysical pun on the family name Sir Gilbert had explained the function of Daybrook: to provide a traditional structure which, so long as it continues, can forestall, by integrating conscious and unconscious modes of awareness, the annihilating flood in which either mode, given dominance, would extinguish both the individual and civilization:

"Nay, . . . though I say that Daybrook is the ark of the Vale, I mean not the house itself, but He that Day, that lives in the house in his day. While Day there be in Daybrook, the floods shall not cover the Vale nor shall they ride over England completely." [p. 781]

In other words, Daybrook is the ark above the flood, ascending to Ararat, as well as the ark of the covenant, reconciling God and man, immortality and mortality, the Greater and the lesser day.

Further elaborating on his meaning, Sir Gilbert had written:

"For the little day is like a house with the family round the hearth, and the door shut. Yet outside whispers the Greater Day, wall-less, and hearthless. And the time will come at last when the walls of the little day shall fall, and what is left of the family of men shall find themselves outdoors in the Greater Day, houseless and abroad, even here between the knees of the Vales, even in Crichdale." [p. 785]

This doom is the common fate of all men, yet there is a difference be·tween the ways in which "little men" and "tall men" confront it: "And little men will shudder and die out," but in the epic simile which gives the story its title,

"Even as the flying fish, when he leaves the air and recovereth his element in the depth, plunges and invisibly rejoices. So will tall men rejoice, after their flight of fear, through the thin air, pursued by death." [pp. 785–786]

Sir Gilbert had elaborated on man's fate and had offered pertinent counsel on how to reconcile oneself to it:

"Thou art a fish in the timeless Ocean, and must needs fall back. Take heed lest thou break thyself in the fall! For death is not in dying, but in the fear. Cease then the struggle of thy flight, and fall back into the deep element where death is and is not, and life is not a fleeing away." [p. 788]

In his illness Gethin Day has hurried "just over the edge": "Now, try as he might, he was aware of a gap in his time-space *continuum;* he was, in the words of his ancestor, aware of the Greater Day showing through the cracks of the ordinary day" (p. 788). Though he feels "used up, worn out," the traditional wisdom of the *Book of Days* offers a solution in the reconciliation of one's own individual span of life with the larger, hidden portion of the cycle:

"Be still, upon the sperm of life, which spills alone in its hour. . . . Be still, upon thine own sun.
  ". . . Thou hast a sun in thee, and it is not timed. Therefore wait. Wait, and be at peace with thine own sun, which is thy sperm of life. Be at peace with thy sun in thee, as the volcano is, and the dark holly-bush before berry-time, and the long hours of night." [p. 789]

In quasi-biblical, prophetic language, the passage continues:

"Take no care, for what thou knowest is ever less than what thou art. The full fire even of thine own sun in thine own body, thou canst never know. So how shouldst thou load care upon thy sun? Take heed, take thought, take pleasure, take pain, take all things as thy sun stirs. Only fasten not thyself in care about anything, for care is impiety, it spits upon the sun." [p. 789]

Gethin Day's call to Daybrook is, then, a summons to integration. Too ill to travel for a time, however, he recuperates in the open air of the town square. The plaza, "like a great low fountain of green and of dark shade," comes vividly alive in imagery suggesting the contrasting modes of experience:

Scarlet, yellow, green, blue-green, sunshine intense and invisible, deep indigo shade! and small, white-clad natives pass, passing, across the square, through the green lawns, under the indigo shade, and across the hollow sunshine of the road into the arched arcades of the low Spanish buildings, where the shops were. [p. 784]

Here where the bells of the squat yellow cathedral sound hollow, "heavy as a strange bell of shadow-coloured glass, the shadow of the greater day hung over this coloured plaza which the Europeans had created, like an oasis, in the lost depths of Mexico" (p. 784).

At the end of the broken, linear thread of the railway which links it to the lesser day of European civilization hangs the town itself, "revolving," in a simile recalling Jonathan Edwards's striking image in *Sinners in the Hands of an Angry God*, "like a spider" in the mythic Greater Day of the valley, "a cleft in the plateau," a "vast, varying declivity of the *barranca*," suggesting the Magna Mater.

The little train on which Gethin Day departs runs "fussily on, in the little day of toys and men's machines," while four small deer gaze impassively from the Greater Day of the ravine. An old beggar woman, in whose voice "the Englishman heard again the fathomless crooning appeal of the Indian women, moaning stranger, more terrible than the ring-dove, with a sadness that had no horizon," personifies the Magna Mater:

Over the door of her womb was written not only: "*Lasciate ogni speranza, voi ch'entrate*," but: "*Perdite ogni pianto, voi ch'uscite*." For the men who had known these women were beyond weeping and beyond even despair, mute in the timeless compulsion of the Greater Day. [pp. 787–788]

But a world in which a woman exists, not as an individual woman, but only as the Magna Mater, is itself a partial world.

Whatever Lawrence's criticism of the one-sided lesser day of white consciousness, this total absorption in the greater day of dark consciousness, he has learned, is as great an imbalance on the other side. The contrast in attitudes in providing public food service for travelers illustrates the opposite kinds of imbalance. On the train, big, handsome Mexican Indian men, absorbed in the Greater Day, "could sell glasses of ice-cream at twenty-five centavos, and not really know they were doing it." At the station, "in the big but forlorn railway restaurant" of the white man's lesser day, the "regular meal . . . came with American mechanical take-it-or-leave-it flatness" (p. 788).

The train, in characteristic Laurentian irony, runs from the Southern town through the Greater Day of the valley to Vera Cruz, "a port of nullity, nihilism concrete and actual, calling itself the city of the True Cross" (p. 790). The German ship on which Gethin Day embarks, curiously anticipating Katherine Anne Porter's S. S. *Vera*, which was to sail from the same port in 1933, is a Laurentian "ship of fools," with its German crew and its passenger list of English, Danish, German, Spanish, and Cuban servants of bourgeois materialism. While Gethin Day resists "the clutches of Mammon's mean day" by traveling second class, two Danish businessmen in the first-class saloon, having been "fêted and feasted, and shown what they were meant to see," fall ill of food poisoning in their inability to incorporate the sensual-sexual connotations of the oysters they have eaten in Vera Cruz (pp. 790–791). As the vessel sails into the Gulf of Mexico, Gethin Day, in an equal if more respectable imbalance on the other side, sits for hours on the phallic bowsprit, lost in contemplation of the creative mystery as the cigar-shaped ship plows through the bright water, turning the spray on either side and starting the flying fish into metaphorical flight of vivid, momentary life:

It was very lovely, and on the softly-lifting bowsprit of the long, swift ship the body was cradled in the sway of timeless life, the soul lay in the jewel-coloured moment, the jewel-pure eternity of this gulf of nowhere.

And always, always, like a dream, the flocks of flying fish swept into the air, from nowhere, and went brilliantly twinkling in their flight of silvery water wings rapidly fluttering, away, low as swallows over the smooth curved surface of the sea, then gone again, vanished, without splash or evidence, gone. One alone like a little silver twinkle. Gone! The sea was still and silky-surfaced, blue and softly heaving, empty, purity itself, sea, sea, sea. [pp. 792–793]

But Gethin Day is alone in his vision. If a ship's officer occasionally peers over the edge and discovers him, "curled in the wonder of this gulf of creation," he says nothing: "People didn't like looking over the edge. It was too beautiful, too pure and lovely, the Greater Day" (p. 793).

On the third morning, Gethin Day sees, in a school of porpoises, the paradoxical image of the changeless reality in the flux of temporal experience. The passage, among Lawrence's most evocative prose, deserves quotation in full:

The porpoises were ten or a dozen, round-bodied torpedo fish, and they stayed there as if they were not moving, always there, with no motion apparent, under the purely pellucid water, yet speeding on just at the speed of the ship without the faintest show of movement, yet speeding on in the most miraculous precision of speed. . . . It seemed as if nothing moved, yet fish and ship swept on through the tropical ocean. And the fish moved, they changed places all the time. They moved in a little cloud, and with the most wonderful sport they were above, they were below, they were to the fore, yet all the time the same one speed, the same one speed, and the last fish just touching with its tail-flukes the iron cut-water of the ship. Some would be down in the blue, shadowy, but horizontally motionless in the same speed. Then with a strange revolution, these would be up in pale green water, and others would be down. Even the toucher, who touched the ship, would in a twinkling, be changed. . . . All the time, so swift, they seemed to be laughing. [p. 794]

Lawrence's description echoes the passage in *The Rime of the Ancient Mariner* where, in Coleridge's gloss, "by the light of the Moon, he beholdeth God's creatures of the great calm" and "blesseth them in his heart":

> Within the shadow of the ship
> I watched their rich attire:
> Blue, glossy green, and velvet black,
> They coiled and swam; and every track
> Was a flash of golden fire.
>
> O happy living things! no tongue
> Their beauty might declare:
> A spring of love gushed from my heart,
> And I blessed them unaware.
>   [ll. 276–285]

Gethin Day, mesmerized by the "joy of life" in the sea creatures, wonders: "What civilization will bring us to such a pitch of swift laughing togetherness, as these fish have reached?" (p. 795).

In juxtaposing the images of the porpoises and the flying fish in relation to the ship, a figure for the creative thrust of consciousness, Lawrence relates, even as he distinguishes between, the concepts of the Greater Day and the lesser day. The porpoises, in their joyous accompaniment of the ship, suggest the dark, instinctual energy of the creative unconscious, characterized not by repressed guilts but by a prelapsarian joy anterior to self-consciousness: "And ever, ever the same pure horizontal speed, sometimes a dark back skimming the water's surface light, from beneath, but never the surface broken" (p. 794). The flying fish, in their tremulous, transitory flight above the surface, suggest the bright, momentaneous soaring of the individual life into a consciousness informed and heightened in beauty by the awareness of death: ". . . the flying fishes on translucent wings swept in their ecstatic clouds out of the water, in a terror that was brilliant as joy, in a joy brilliant with terror, with wings made of pure water flapping with great speed, and long-shafted bodies of translucent silver like squirts of living water, there in air, brilliant in air, before suddenly they had disappeared, and the blue sea was trembling with a delicate surface of green . . ." (p. 793).

In the last section that Lawrence wrote of the fragment the ship stops in Cuba before moving on to the Atlantic crossing. In rude contrast to the Greater Day in which the fish twinkle with vivid life, Havana is vulgar and Americanized, exploited in the capitalistic prostitution of the lesser day. A chauffeur tells Gethin Day: "'Ah, *los americanos!* They are so good. You know they own us. They own Havana. We are a Republic owned by the Americans. *Muy bien,* we give them drink, they give us money. Bah!'" (p. 796). Since the American *turistas* lose consciousness only in alcohol, they reduce their identities to signs, wearing badges designating name and hotel so that when they are found insensible on the street, the police can cart them home.

The expensive Havana cemetery, with its fifty-thousand-dollar monuments, contrasts strikingly with the grave of the Atlantic, "where the bright, lost world of Atlantis is buried." The Atlantic crossing, like the voyage in *St. Mawr,* is a ritual passage from one kind of being to another. But whereas Lou Witt's crossing was a voyage out, the first leg on a journey of separation, Gethin Day's is a voyage back, a return to reintegration. Yet the passage is a difficult one, marked by violent opposite motions: "The narrow cigar of a ship heaved up the upslope with a nauseating heave, up, up, up, till she righted for a second sickeningly on the top, then tilted. . . . Then down she slid, down the long, shivering downslope . . ." (p. 797). In his seasickness, Gethin Day experiences the full shock of re-entry. On the third day, with the return threshold crossed, the healing rain begins to fall and the motion subsides.

It is here that the fragment ends. When Lawrence read the unfinished manuscript to Earl and Achsah Brewster in Switzerland in 1928, they urged him to complete the story; but he replied that the fragment was "'written so near the borderline of death, that I have never been able to carry it through in the cold light of day.'" Lawrence told the Brewsters that "the last part will be regenerate man, a real life in this Garden of Eden,"[5] a plan which was never carried out in the imagined terms of "The Flying Fish" but which was realized in part, in a somewhat different version, in *The Man Who Died*.

TOWARD RECONCILIATION

The aboriginal ground of America came closer than any other earthly place to embodying the "place" of Lawrence's vision. But if, as he insists, "New Mexico was the greatest experience from the outside world that I ever had" (*Phoenix*, p. 142), the question of why he left it to return to Europe remains to be answered. The reason is to be found, I believe, in the complex of motives and experience representing a major transformation which was taking place in Lawrence's life.

Lawrence's serious illness of the winter of 1925 was perhaps his deepest descent into his own primordial unconscious, lying deeper than sex, beyond choice, where the ultimate distinction is between organic life and death. Yet, as Joseph Campbell says of the monomythic hero:

His consciousness having succumbed, the unconscious nevertheless supplies its own balance, and he is born back into the world from which he came. Instead of holding to and saving his ego, . . . he loses it, and yet, through grace, it is returned.

In the last section he wrote of "The Flying Fish," Lawrence encounters the final crisis of his quest, "the paradoxical, supremely difficult threshold-crossing of the hero's return from the mystic realm into the land of common day":

. . . he has yet to re-enter with his boon the long-forgotten atmosphere where men who are fractions imagine themselves to be complete. He has yet to confront society with his ego-shattering, life-redeeming elixir. . . .[6]

If there is a real danger that, on the hero's return, the cosmic vision of the center may give way to "the peripheral crisis of the moment," there is also, in Lawrence's case, an even greater danger that, tempted by "the soul-satisfying vision of fulfillment" to linger in the transcendent reality of the other world, he may reject as unreal the temporal joys and sorrows of the mundane world, which it has been his quest to redeem. In "The Flying Fish" he confronts the first task of the hero on reentry, that of trying to reconcile the paradoxical wisdom brought from the unconscious deep with the prudential concerns of consciousness.[7]

Throughout his wander years, Lawrence has come to realize he has been projecting upon the world his own inner needs. It is as if he has been saying, "I could be whole if I could unite with the organic cycle of nature, descend into darkness to embrace the Great Mother, then emerge to establish Rananim, and so encounter in the new environment all that is lacking in the mechanistic halfness of western civilization." Such needs, arising from the unconscious, emerge into consciousness as images of the sort which Susanne K. Langer calls "presentational symbols" not easily translated into discursive language.[8] Lawrence, unfortunately for his art, has literalized these metaphors in the militarily enforced religious revival of *The Plumed Serpent*. As Campbell affirms:

> Symbols are only the *vehicles* of communication; they must not be mistaken for the final term, the *tenor,* of their reference. No matter how attractive or impressive they may seem, they remain but convenient means, accommodated to the understanding. . . . The problem of the theologian is to keep his symbol translucent, so that it may not block out the very light it is supposed to convey. . . . Mistaking a vehicle for its tenor may lead to the spilling not only of valueless ink, but of valuable blood.[9]

And that is precisely what it does in *The Plumed Serpent*. Already in *Kangaroo* Lawrence had rejected Prime Minister Lloyd George's brand of democracy in the England of the chapter called "The Nightmare," as well as the perfectionist schemes of Ben Cooley's fascism and Willie Struthers's socialism in the fictional Australia of the novel. Finally, because an organic utopian order established upon a religious and political orthodoxy is patently a contradiction in values rather than a reconciliation of opposites, Lawrence must also reject even Don Ramón Carrasco's theocracy, which cannot be effected without violating others by an act of one's own will, as little more satisfactory for organizing society and engendering individual creativity than the political systems he has rejected earlier.

In the relinquishment of his dream of Rananim, in the glimpse of death in his serious illness, in the very process of aging into middle life, Lawrence became aware of other problems than he had faced before. In his discussion of the progressive balancing of psychic forces which he calls "centroversion," Carl G. Jung amplifies the traditional analogy between man's life and the daily course of the sun: at noon "the descent begins" and with it "the reversal of all the ideals and values that were cherished in the morning."[10] As Erich Neumann expresses it:

We can say, then, that with the phenomenon of the second half of life the personal development of centroversion enters upon a second phase. Whereas its initial phase led to the development of the ego and to the differentiation of the psychic system, its second phase brings development of the self and the integration of that system.

In most persons, the first half of life is characterized by "progressive mastery of the world and adaptation to it." Lawrence, like most creative individuals, experienced, even during that period of his life, "a surcharge of unconscious activity," which he adapted to the conscious, structuring process of his art. As Neumann elaborates:

In the integration process the personality goes back along the path it took during the phase of differentiation. It is now a question of reaching a synthesis between the conscious mind and the psyche as a whole, that is, between the ego and the self, so that a new wholeness may be constellated between the hitherto diametrically opposed systems of conscious and unconscious.[11]

Rather than renouncing the values which he had partly sought and partly projected in America, Lawrence, at about the age of forty, began to integrate them in the larger system of the individualized self.

The fact that Rananim could be founded only temporarily, and with less success than one might wish, between the covers of *The Plumed Serpent* does not invalidate the prelapsarian state as literary symbol. In his later work, however, Lawrence shifts the value of the symbol from the societal to the individual sphere. "The Flying Fish," fragmentary though it may be, is a pivotal work in Lawrence's canon because it is centered in a transformational stage in his personal development. From this point on, the energy which he had expended in search of the place or society through which the individual might be regenerated is invested in the integration of the individual in personal terms.

The difference this transformation makes in Lawrence's fiction may be seen in his contrasting resolutions of the love relationships in *Women in Love* (1920), written just before his wander years, and *Lady Chatterley's Lover* (1928), written just after them. In *Women in Love,* Birkin and Ursula, in their "star equilibrium," have their little "chink" of the world, set apart from the "market-places and street corners" where the meek servants of money will "inherit the earth." But Birkin is plagued by a need to "wander about on the face of the earth," to "look at the world beyond just this bit": " 'You see,' he said, 'I always imagine our being really happy with some few other people —a little freedom with people.' " Ursula's reply is prophetic:

"Why should you *need* others? Why must you force people to agree with you? Why can't you be single by yourself, as you are always saying? . . . You've got me. And yet you want to force other people to love you as well. You do try to bully them to love you. And even then you don't want their love." [pp. 353–355]

With the candle flame from Gerald Crich's bier flickering coldly between them, Birkin and Ursula subsequently reiterate the same positions. " 'You can't have two kinds of love,' " she insists at the end of the novel, " '. . . because it's false, impossible.' " " 'I don't believe that,' " Birkin declares (pp. 472–473).

In *Lady Chatterley's Lover,* on the other hand, Mellors and Connie, though separated geographically, have achieved, in the tenderness of their sexual relationship, a world beyond money, beyond even Rananim. The transformation is clear in their plan that "for six months he should work at farming, so that eventually he and Connie could have some small farm of their own, into which he could put his energy" (p. 360). Though the industrial waste land encroaches further and further upon their forest-garden, they require no more world than the love-saints of John Donne's "The Canonization," ". . . whom reverend love/Made one anothers hermitage" (lines 37–38):

> We'are Tapers too, and at our owne cost die,
>   And wee in us finde the'Eagle and the Dove.
> The Phoenix ridle hath more wit
>   By us, we two being one, are it.
>
> [ll. 21–24]

Ultimately wiser than Birkin, Mellors, in imagery reminiscent of Donne's, evokes "the forked flame":

"You can't insure against the future, except by really believing in the best bit of you, and in the power beyond it. So I believe in the little flame between us. For me now, it's the only thing in the world. I've got no friends, not inward friends. Only you. And now the little flame is all I care about in my life." [p. 364]

They have, like Donne's love-saints, so fully reconciled sacred and profane love that Mellors can even declare in his separation from Connie: "So I love chastity now, because it is the peace that comes of fucking" (p. 364).

What Lawrence has come to realize is that the redeeming qualities of the dark consciousness, which aboriginal America embodied for him, are not to be projected outward in the form of grandiose schemes for world regeneration but integrated in the individuation of consciousness within the self. With this knowledge, he must close the circle of his American quest by taking the long arc back to pick up the thread of his own cultural tradition. For in identifying himself with the larger context of western civilization, he can, paradoxically, both move toward a new synthesis of the self and accept the ultimate renunciation of individual identity in the dissolution of death, an experience which he has already begun to incorporate imaginatively in "The Flying Fish."

If culture and wisdom, as Jung suggests, are to be "the meaning and purpose of the second half of life,"[12] the synthesis of conscious and unconscious modes of experience represented in these qualities has the function psychologically, and spiritually, of preparing the individual for his confrontation with death. Erik Erikson sees the psychological task of maturity as a resolution of the conflict between ego integrity and despair. Because it is particularly relevant to an understanding of the moral issues which impelled Lawrence's return to Europe, Erikson's concept of ego integrity requires elaboration. "It is," he says, "a postnarcissistic love of the human ego—not of the self—as an experience which conveys some world order and spiritual sense. . . . It is the acceptance of one's one and only life cycle as something that had to be and that, by necessity, permitted of no substitutions." The goal of ego integrity means, then, a reorientation in one's relation to the past: "a new, a different love of one's parents," "a comradeship with the ordering ways of distant times and different pursuits." At the same time, it means an affirmation of the dignity and worth of one's own life style. Since "an individual life is the accidental coincidence of but one life cycle with but one segment of history," one knows "that for him all human integrity stands or falls with the one style of integrity of which he partakes. The style of integrity developed by his culture or civilization thus becomes the 'patrimony of his soul,' the seal of his moral paternity of himself. . . ." "In such final consolidation," Erikson concludes, "death loses its sting."[13] Ego integrity, of course, is a dynamic process, not a monolithic condition. Its achievement, therefore, must be, for anyone, relative rather than static.

The four and a half years following Lawrence's return from America were years of struggle, both physical and moral, with the necessity to encompass imaginatively the knowledge and experience of his own death. "The Ship of Death" and the cluster of shorter poems related to it "all fit together," Richard Aldington says, as if intended to make a single poem, "and in all of them suffering and the agony of departure are turned into music and reconciliation. . . ."[14] The myth in which Lawrence's meditation on death is structurally and thematically centered is, significantly, not the blood sacrifice of the Aztecs but the funeral customs of the ancients along the Mediterranean. These customs, as Elizabeth Cipolla suggests, represented for the ancients, not mere piety toward the dead, but the moral qualities of life. Thus, in Lawrence's poem, "the building of the ship is an act of faith, the committing of the soul to the dark flood is an act of courage," the same moral qualities which, having been "painfully cultivated throughout a lifetime," enable one "to die with dignity and serenity." In this cultural context, "dying is not passively suffered but is instead an experience which the whole man encounters, senses and mind alert, accepting the pain as a necessary part of the adventure."[15]

If "The Ship of Death" encompasses the entire triad of the *felix culpa*—life, death, and rebirth—Lawrence, in two of his last works, *The Man Who Died* (1929) and "The Risen Lord" (1929), delineates the pattern of the third movement of the cycle. In *The Man Who Died*, Lawrence realizes imaginatively the quest of the post-Christian hero. In the image of the escaped cock with which the narrative begins, Lawrence foreshadows the risen man's freeing himself not only from the bonds of death but also from the fetters of idealism, the subjugation of the sensual to the dominance of the spiritual. Lawrence's mythic strategy is twofold: first, drawing a reverse parallel between the New Testament accounts of Jesus' life and this version of the man's life after his resurrection, Lawrence alters the meaning of numerous scriptural allusions by shifting them from the spiritual context of the authorized gospels to the sensual context of his fable. Second, in the sexual union of the risen man and the priestess of Isis, who serves the goddess in her search for the lost phallus of the slain and mutilated Osiris, Lawrence syncretizes the Christian and Egyptian myths. Both Christ and Osiris performed miracles of fertility, the one converting water into wine and the other introducing the treading of grapes; and both, more significantly, were betrayed by "brothers," slain, and deified.[16] Their identification is complete when the risen man, tumescent with the lost phallicism of Osiris, utters, as

Julian Moynahan calls it, "the baroque conceit"[17] of "I am risen!" (p. 43). The mythic lovers are redeemed, but the world, as in *Lady Chatterley's Lover,* is fallen still. The priestess's mother and her slaves force the risen man's departure; yet from the new perspective which consolidates the hitherto separate truths of sensual and spiritual love, he can view them as "little people" of the "little day" and adhere to the new gospel: "Unless we encompass it in the greater day, and set the little life in the circle of the greater life, all is disaster" (p. 36). Secure in the faith that, in the reconciliation between mythic and linear time, the cycle is unremitting, he takes leave of the priestess with a sensual paraphrase of his biblical promise: "And when the nightingale calls again from your valley-bed, I shall come again, sure as spring" (p. 46).[18]

Identified at the end of *The Man Who Died* with the natural cycle, the risen man becomes a "lord" in an important essay written in July 1929, only a few months before Lawrence's death, as a coda to the short novel. In "The Risen Lord" Lawrence again castigates the Church for the halfness of its Christian message:

The Churches loudly assert: We preach Christ crucified!—But in so doing, they preach only half of the Passion, and do only half their duty. The Creed says: "Was crucified, dead, and buried . . . the third day He rose again from the dead." And again, I believe in the resurrection of the body. . . ." So that to preach Christ Crucified is to preach half the truth. It is the business of the Church to preach Christ born among men—which is Christmas; Christ crucified, which is Good Friday; and Christ Risen, which is Easter. And after Easter, till November and All Saints, and till Annunciation, the year belongs to the Risen Lord: that is, all the full-flowering spring, all summer, and the autumn of wheat and fruit, all belong to Christ Risen. [*Phoenix II,* p. 571]

With the reminder that "the great religious images are only images of our own experiences," Lawrence invokes a risen Jesus who can take up carpentry again, embrace a man in friendship and a woman in sexual tenderness, beget children in love, and announce to the startled Tempter: "Satan, your silly temptations no longer tempt me" (pp. 575–576):

If Jesus rose from the dead in triumph, a man on earth triumphant in renewed flesh, triumphant over the mechanical anti-life convention of Jewish priests, Roman despotism, and universal money-lust; triumphant above all over His own self-absorption, self-consciousness, self-importance; triumphant and free as a man in full flesh and full, final experience, even the accomplished acceptance of His own death; a man at last full and free in flesh and soul, a man at one with death: then He rose to become at one with life, to live the great life of the flesh and the soul together, as peonies or foxes do, in their lesser way. [*Phoenix II*, p. 575]

Lawrence's postscript to a letter to Maria Huxley, written from Ad Astra, Vence ("Friday," 21 February 1930), as Mark Schorer once noted,[19] was, in terms of his search for a place, highly connotative: "This place no good." But in terms of his religious quest, the postscript to his subsequent letter to E. H. Brewster ("Thursday," probably 27 February 1930), referring to the clay head Jo Davidson had just made of him, is even more suggestive; nearly the last words Lawrence wrote were ". . . result in clay mediocre."

For Lawrence's commitment to a reconciliation between flesh and spirit, pagan and Christian in a new, syncretic religious order is the basis for his ultimate faith that in the reborn man the kingdom of the Holy Ghost is at hand.

NOTES

1. *Dark Night of the Body: D. H. Lawrence's "The Plumed Serpent"* (Austin: University of Texas Press, 1964), p. 13.

2. Harry T. Moore, *The Intelligent Heart: The Story of D. H. Lawrence* (New York: Farrar, Straus, and Young, 1954), p. 340.

3. An exception is Keith Sagar, *The Art of D. H. Lawrence* (Cambridge: Cambridge University Press, 1966), pp. 205–210.

4. Moore, *The Intelligent Heart*, p. 338.

5. Ibid., pp. 338–339.

6. Joseph Campbell, *The Hero with a Thousand Faces*, The Bollingen Series XVII (New York: Pantheon Books, Inc., 1949), p. 216.

7. Ibid., p. 218.

8. *Philosophy in a New Key* (New York: The New American Library, Mentor Book Edition, 1956), p. 79.

9. *The Hero with a Thousand Faces*, p. 236.

10. Carl G. Jung, "The Stages of Life," in *The Structure and Dynamics of the Psyche*, The Bollingen Series XX (New York: Pantheon Books, Inc., 1960), p. 397.

11. *The Origins and History of Consciousness* (New York: Pantheon Books, Inc., 1964), pp. 410–412.

12. "The Stages of Life," p. 400.

13. *Childhood and Society,* 2d ed. rev. (New York: W. W. Norton and Co. Inc., 1963), p. 268. As the context indicates, Erikson's use of the terms *ego* and *self* is not the same as Jung's.

14. "Introduction" to *Last Poems,* in *The Complete Poems of D. H. Lawrence,* II (New York: The Viking Press, 1964), 597–598.

15. "The *Last Poems* of D. H. Lawrence," *The D. H. Lawrence Review,* II (Summer, 1969), 112, 114.

16. See Sir James George Frazer, *The Golden Bough: A Study in Magic and Religion,* 1 vol., abridged ed. (New York: The Macmillan Co., 1951), pp. 420–447.

17. *The Deed of Life: The Novels and Tales of D. H. Lawrence* (Princeton: Princeton University Press, 1963), p. 178.

18 For a more extensive treatment of both of Lawrence's mythic strategies in the short novel, see my essay "The Function of Allusions and Symbols in D. H. Lawrence's *The Man Who Died," The American Imago,* XVII (Fall, 1960), 241–253.

19. "Introduction" to Harry T. Moore, *Poste Restante: A Lawrence Travel Calendar* (Berkeley and Los Angeles: University of California Press, 1956), p. 18.

List of Works Cited

WORKS BY D. H. LAWRENCE

Lawrence, D. H. *Apocalypse*. Introduction by Richard Aldington. New York: The Viking Press, Compass Book, 1966.

——. *The Collected Letters of D. H. Lawrence*. 2 vols. Edited and with Introduction by Harry T. Moore. New York: The Viking Press, 1962.

——. *The Complete Poems of D. H. Lawrence*. 2 vols. Edited by Vivian de Sola Pinto and Warren Roberts. New York: The Viking Press, 1964.

——. *The Complete Short Stories of D. H. Lawrence*. 3 vols. Melbourne, London, Toronto: William Heinemann Ltd., 1955; New York: The Viking Press, Compass Book, 1966.

——. *Kangaroo*. Melbourne, London, Toronto: William Heinemann Ltd., 1955; The Viking Press, Compass Book, 1966.

——. *Lady Chatterley's Lover*. 1st Authorized Unexpurgated Edition. Introduction by Mark Schorer. New York: Grove Press, Inc., 1959.

——. *The Later D. H. Lawrence*. Selected, with Introduction by William York Tindall. New York: Alfred A. Knopf, 1952.

——. *The Letters of D. H. Lawrence*. Edited and with Introduction by Aldous Huxley. New York: The Viking Press, 1936.

——. *Mornings in Mexico* and *Etruscan Places*. Vol. III of *The Travel Books of D. H. Lawrence*. Melbourne, London, Toronto: William Heinemann Ltd., 1956.

——. *Movements in European History*. Oxford: Oxford University Press, Humphrey Milford, 1925.

——. *Phoenix: The Posthumous Papers of D. H. Lawrence*. Edited and with Introduction by Edward D. McDonald. New York: The Viking Press, 1968.

——. *Phoenix II: Uncollected, Unpublished, and Other Prose Works by D. H. Lawrence*. Edited and with Introduction by Warren Roberts and Harry T. Moore. New York: The Viking Press, 1968.

——. *The Plumed Serpent*. Melbourne, London, Toronto: William Heinemann Ltd., 1962.

——. *Psychoanalysis and the Unconscious* and *Fantasia of the Unconscious*. Introduction by Philip Rieff. New York: The Viking Press, Compass Book, 1960.

————. *The Rainbow*. Melbourne, London, Toronto: William Heinemann Ltd., 1957; New York: The Viking Press, Compass Book, 1966.

————. *Sea and Sardinia*. Introduction by Richard Aldington. New York: The Viking Press, Compass Book, 1963.

————. *The Short Novels of D. H. Lawrence*. 2 vols. Melbourne, London, Toronto: William Heinemann Ltd., 1956.

————. *Sons and Lovers*. New York: The Viking Press, Compass Book, 1966.

————. *Studies in Classic American Literature*. New York: The Viking Press, Compass Book, 1966.

————. *The Symbolic Meaning: The Uncollected Versions of "Studies in Classic American Literature."* Edited with Introduction by Armin Arnold. New York: The Viking Press, 1964.

————. *Twilight in Italy*. New York: The Viking Press, 1958.

————. *Women in Love*. Melbourne, London, Toronto: William Heinemann Ltd., 1957; New York: Compass Book, 1966.

STUDIES OF D. H. LAWRENCE AND HIS WORKS

BIOGRAPHICAL STUDIES

Brett, Dorothy. *Lawrence and Brett: A Friendship*. Philadelphia: J. B. Lippincott Co., 1933.

Carswell, Catherine. *The Savage Pilgrimage: A Narrative of D. H. Lawrence*. London: Chatto and Windus, 1932.

Lawrence, Frieda. *Frieda Lawrence: The Memoirs and Correspondence*. Edited and with Preface by E. W. Tedlock, Jr. New York: Alfred A. Knopf, 1964.

————. *"Not I But the Wind . . ."* . New York: The Viking Press, 1934.

Luhan, Mabel Dodge. *Lorenzo in Taos*. New York: Alfred A. Knopf, 1932.

Merrild, Knud. *A Poet and Two Painters: A Memoir of D. H. Lawrence*. New York: The Viking Press, 1939.

Moore, Harry T. *D. H. Lawrence: His Life and Works*. rev. ed. New York: Twayne Publishers, Inc., 1964.

————. *The Intelligent Heart: The Story of D. H. Lawrence*. New York: Farrar, Straus, and Young, Inc., 1954.

————. *Poste Restante: A Lawrence Travel Calendar*. Introduction by Mark Schorer. Berkeley and Los Angeles: University of California Press, 1956.

Murry, John Middleton. *Reminiscences of D. H. Lawrence*. New York: Henry Holt and Co., 1933.

Nehls, Edward, ed. *D. H. Lawrence: A Composite Biography*. 3 vols. Madison: University of Wisconsin Press, 1957–1959.

CRITICAL STUDIES

Books

Arnold, Armin. *D. H. Lawrence and America.* New York: Philosophical Library, Inc., 1959.

Beal, Anthony. *D. H. Lawrence.* Writers and Critics. Edinburgh and London: Oliver and Boyd, 1961.

Clark, L. D. *Dark Night of the Body: D. H. Lawrence's "The Plumed Serpent."* Photographs by LaVerne Harrell Clark. Austin: University of Texas Press, 1964.

Daleski, H. M. *The Forked Flame: A Study of D. H. Lawrence.* Evanston, Ill.: Northwestern University Press, 1965.

Draper, R. P. *D. H. Lawrence.* New York: Twayne Publishers, Inc., 1964.

Ford, George H. *Double Measure: A Study of the Novels and Stories of D. H. Lawrence.* New York, Chicago, San Francisco: Holt, Rinehart, and Winston, 1965.

Freeman, Mary. *D. H. Lawrence: A Basic Study of His Ideas.* Gainesville, Fla.: University of Florida Press, 1955.

Goodheart, Eugene. *The Utopian Vision of D. H. Lawrence.* Chicago: University of Chicago Press, 1963.

Gordon, David J. *D. H. Lawrence as a Literary Critic.* New Haven and London: Yale University Press, 1966.

Gregory, Horace. *D. H. Lawrence: Pilgrim of the Apocalypse, A Critical Study.* New York: Grove Press, Inc., Evergreen Books Edition, 1957.

Hoffman, Frederick J., and Harry T. Moore, eds. *The Achievement of D. H. Lawrence.* Norman: University of Oklahoma Press, 1953.

Hough, Graham. *The Dark Sun: A Study of D. H. Lawrence.* New York: The Macmillan Co., 1957.

Leavis, F. R. *D. H. Lawrence: Novelist.* New York: Alfred A. Knopf, 1956.

Moore, Harry T., ed. *A D. H. Lawrence Miscellany.* Carbondale, Ill.: Southern Illinois University Press, 1959.

Moynahan, Julian. *The Deed of Life: The Novels and Tales of D. H. Lawrence.* Princeton: Princeton University Press, 1963.

Rieff, Philip. *The Triumph of the Therapeutic: Uses of Faith after Freud.* New York: Harper and Row, 1966.

Sagar, Keith. *The Art of D. H. Lawrence.* Cambridge: Cambridge University Press, 1966.

Spilka, Mark, ed. *D. H. Lawrence: A Collection of Critical Essays.* Twentieth Century Views. Englewood Cliffs, N.J.: Prentice-Hall, Inc., 1963.

————. *The Love Ethic of D. H. Lawrence.* Bloomington: Indiana University Press, Midland Book, 1957.

Tedlock, E. W., Jr., ed. *D. H. Lawrence and "Sons and Lovers": Sources and Criticism.* New York: New York University Press, 1965.

————. *D. H. Lawrence: Artist and Rebel: A Study of Lawrence's Fiction.* Albuquerque: University of New Mexico Press, 1963.

Tindall, William York. *D. H. Lawrence and Susan His Cow.* New York: Columbia University Press, 1939.

Tiverton, Father William [Jarrett-Kerr, Father Martin]. *D. H. Lawrence and Human Existence.* Foreword by T. S. Eliot. London: Rockliff, 1951.

Vivas, Eliseo. *D. H. Lawrence: The Failure and the Triumph of Art.* London: George Allen and Unwin Ltd., 1961.

Weiss, Daniel A. *Oedipus in Nottingham: D. H. Lawrence.* Seattle: University of Washington Press, 1962.

West, Anthony. *D. H. Lawrence.* 2d ed. London: Arthur Barker Ltd., 1966.

Widmer, Kingsley. *The Art of Perversity: D. H. Lawrence's Shorter Fictions.* Seattle: University of Washington Press, 1962.

Young, Kenneth. *D. H. Lawrence.* Writers and Their Work, No. 31. London, New York, Toronto: Published for the British Council by Longmans, Green and Co., 1956.

Articles

Cipolla, Elizabeth. "The *Last Poems* of D. H. Lawrence," *The D. H. Lawrence Review,* II (1969), 103–119.

Cowan, James C. "The Function of Allusions and Symbols in D. H. Lawrence's *The Man Who Died,*" *The American Imago,* XVII (1960), 241–253.

Daleski, H. M. "The Duality of Lawrence," *Modern Fiction Studies,* V (Spring, 1959), 3–18.

Fergusson, Francis. "D. H. Lawrence's Sensibility." In *Critiques and Essays on Modern Fiction, 1920–1951.* Edited by John W. Aldridge, pp. 328–339. New York: The Ronald Press Co., 1952.

Isaacs, Neil D. "The Autoerotic Metaphor in Joyce, Sterne, Lawrence, Stevens, and Whitman," *Literature and Psychology,* XV (Spring, 1965), 92–106.

Liddell, Robert. "Lawrence and Dr. Leavis: The Case of *St. Mawr,*" *Essays in Criticism,* IV (July, 1954), 321–327. Replies by David Craig, Mark Roberts, and T. W. Thomas in "Critical Forum," *Essays in Criticism,* V (January, 1955), 64–80.

Merivale, Patricia. "D. H. Lawrence and the Modern Pan Myth," *Texas Studies in Literature and Language,* VI (1964), 296–305

New, William H. "Character as Symbol: Annie's Role in *Sons and Lovers,*" *The D. H. Lawrence Review,* I (Spring, 1968), 31–43.

Vickery, John B. "Myth and Ritual in the Shorter Fiction of D. H. Lawrence," *Modern Fiction Studies,* V (Spring, 1959), 65–82.

————. "*The Plumed Serpent* and the Eternal Paradox," *Criticism,* V (1963), 119–134.

Whitaker, Thomas R. "Lawrence's Western Path: 'Mornings in Mexico,'"
    Criticism, III (1961), 219–236.
Wilde, Alan. "The Illusion of *St. Mawr*: Technique and Vision in D. H.
    Lawrence's Novel," *PMLA,* LXXIX (March, 1964), 164–170.

STUDIES IN RELIGION, MYTH, AND RITUAL

Bibby, Geoffrey. *Four Thousand Years Ago: A World Panorama of Life in
    the Second Millennium* B.C. New York: Alfred A. Knopf, 1956.
Campbell, Joseph. *The Hero with a Thousand Faces.* The Bollingen Series
    XVII. New York: Pantheon Books, Inc., 1949.
————. *The Masks of God: Occidental Mythology.* New York: The Viking
    Press, 1964.
————. *The Masks of God: Primitive Mythology.* New York: The Viking
    Press, 1959.
Caso, Alfonso. *The Aztecs: People of the Sun.* Translated by Lowell Dun-
    ham. Norman: University of Oklahoma Press, 1958.
Eliade, Mircea. *Cosmos and History: The Myth of the Eternal Return.*
    Translated by Willard R. Trask. New York: Harper and Brothers,
    Harper Torchbooks, 1959.
Frazer, Sir James George. *The Golden Bough: A Study in Magic and Reli-
    gion.* Abridged ed. 1 vol. New York: The Macmillan Co., 1951.
————. *Totemism and Exogamy: A Treatise on Certain Early Forms of
    Superstition and Society.* 4 vols. London: Macmillan and Co., Ltd.,
    1935.
Graves, Robert. *The White Goddess: A Historical Grammar of Poetic Myth.*
    Amended and enlarged ed. New York: Vintage Books, 1958.
Grimm, The Brothers. *Grimms' Fairy Tales.* Translated by Mrs. E. V. Lucas,
    Lucy Crane, and Marian Edwards. New York: Grosset and Dunlap,
    1945.
Hagen, Victor W. von. *The Ancient Sun Kingdoms of the Americas.* Cleve-
    land and New York: World Publishing Co., 1961.
The Holy Bible. Authorized King James Version.
James, E. O. *The Ancient Gods: The History and Diffusion of Religion in
    the Ancient Near East and the Eastern Mediterranean.* The Putnam
    History of Religion. New York: G. P. Putnam's Sons, 1960.
Kittredge, George Lyman. *Witchcraft in Old and New England.* New York:
    Russell and Russell, Inc., 1958.
Larousse Encyclopedia of Mythology. Introduction by Robert Graves. New
    York: Prometheus Press, 1959.
Michelet, Jules. *Satanism and Witchcraft: A Study in Medieval Superstition.*
    Translated by A. R. Allinson. New York: The Citadel Press, 1939.
Murray, Henry A., ed. *Myth and Mythmaking.* New York: George Braziller,
    1960.

Neumann, Erich. *The Great Mother: An Analysis of the Archetype.* Translated by Ralph Manheim. Bollingen Series XLVII. New York: Pantheon Books, Inc., 1955.

———. *The Origins and History of Consciousness.* Translated by R. F. C. Hull. Bollingen Series XLII. New York: Pantheon Books, Inc., 1964.

Nicholson, Irene. *Firefly in the Night: A Study of Ancient Mexican Poetry and Symbolism.* London: Faber and Faber, 1959.

Olcott, William Tyler. *Sun Lore of All Ages: A Collection of Myths and Legends Concerning the Sun and Its Worship.* New York: G. P. Putnam's Sons, 1914.

Séjourné, Laurette. *Burning Water: Thought and Religion in Ancient Mexico.* London and New York: Thames and Hudson, 1956.

Watts, Alan W. *Myth and Ritual in Christianity.* New York: Grove Press, Inc., 1960.

Zimmer, Heinrich. *The King and the Corpse: Tales of the Soul's Conquest of Evil.* Edited by Joseph Campbell. The Bollingen Series XI. New York: Pantheon Books, Inc., 1948.

OTHER SOURCES

BOOKS

Arieti, Silvano, ed. *American Handbook of Psychiatry.* Vol. I. New York: Basic Books, Inc., 1959.

Coffman, Stanley K., Jr. *Imagism: A Chapter for the History of Modern Poetry.* Norman: University of Oklahoma Press, 1951.

Coleridge, Samuel Taylor. *Selected Poetry and Prose.* Edited and with Introduction and Notes by Elisabeth Schneider. New York: Rinehart and Co., Inc., 1956.

Donne, John. *The Complete Poetry and Selected Prose of John Donne.* Edited and with Introduction by Charles M. Coffin. New York: Random House, The Modern Library, 1952.

Eliot, T. S. *The Complete Poems and Plays, 1909–1950.* New York: Harcourt, Brace and Co., 1952.

English, Horace B., and Ava Champney English. *A Comprehensive Dictionary of Psychological and Psychoanalytic Terms.* New York, London, and Toronto: Longsman, Green and Co., 1958.

Erikson, Erik H. *Childhood and Society.* 2d ed., rev. New York: W. W. Norton and Co., Inc., 1963.

Freud, Sigmund. *The Complete Psychological Works of Sigmund Freud.* Vol. VII: *A Case of Hysteria, Three Essays on Sexuality, and Other Works.* Vol. XIII: *Totem and Taboo and Other Works.* Translated and edited by James Strachey in collaboration with Anna Freud. London: The Hogarth Press and The Institute of Psycho-Analysis, 1953–1955.

Gray, Henry. *Anatomy of the Human Body.* Edited by Warren H. Lewis. 20th ed., rev. Philadelphia and New York: Lea and Febiger, 1918.

Hall, Calvin S. *A Primer of Freudian Psychology.* New York: The New American Library, Mentor Book Edition, 1957.

Hall, Calvin S., and Gardner Lindzey. *Theories of Personality.* New York: John Wiley and Sons, Inc., 1957.

Hoffman, Frederick J. *Freudianism and the Literary Mind.* 2d ed., rev. Baton Rouge: Louisiana State University Press, 1957.

Huxley, Aldous. *Brave New World Revisited.* New York: Harper and Brothers, 1958.

Jung. C. G. *The Collected Works of C. G. Jung.* The Bollingen Series XX. Vol. VIII: *The Structure and Dynamics of the Psyche: Including* "Synchronicity: An Acausal Connecting Principle." Vol. XVI: *The Practice of Psychotherapy: Essays on the Psychology of the Transference and Other Subjects.* 2d ed., rev. Edited by Sir Herbert Read, Michael Fordham, and Gerhard Adler. Translated by R. F. C. Hull. Bollingen Series XX. New York: Pantheon Books, Inc., 1960, 1966.

Langer, Susanne K. *Feeling and Form.* New York: Charles Scribner's Sons, 1953.

————. *Philosophy in a New Key.* New York: The New American Library, Mentor Book Edition, 1956.

Lea, F. A. *The Life of John Middleton Murry.* London: Methuen and Co. Ltd., 1959.

Milton, John. *Complete Poems and Major Prose.* Edited and with Introduction and Notes by Merritt Y. Hughes. New York: The Odyssey Press, 1957.

Munroe, Ruth L. *Schools of Psychoanalytic Thought.* New York: The Dryden Press, Inc., 1956.

Peckham, Morse, ed. *Romanticism: The Culture of the Nineteenth Century.* New York: George Braziller, 1965.

Toynbee, Arnold J. *Civilization on Trial.* New York: Oxford University Press, 1948.

Whitman, Walt. *Leaves of Grass and Selected Prose.* Edited and with Introduction by John Kouwenhoven. New York: Random House, The Modern Library, 1950.

Wolfe, Thomas. *Only the Dead Know Brooklyn.* New York: The New American Library, Signet Books, 1952.

Wordsworth, William. *The Poetical Works of William Wordsworth.* Edited by Thomas Hutchinson. London: Oxford University Press, 1950.

ARTICLES

Peckman, Morse. "Toward a Theory of Romanticism," *PMLA,* LXVI (March, 1951), 5–23.

————. "Toward a Theory of Romanticism II: Reconsiderations," *Studies in Romanticism*, I (Autumn, 1961), 1–8.

Reik, Theodor. "The Three Women in a Man's Life." In *Art and Psychoanalysis*. Edited and with Introduction by William Phillips, pp. 151–164. New York: Criterion Books, 1957.

Index

This index lists textual references to the works of D. H. Lawrence, authors of secondary materials and other actual persons, place names, myths, and subjects. Lawrence's works are indexed alphabetically by title, and secondary materials alphabetically by author. The "letters of D. H. Lawrence" are listed under both that designation and the names of addressees. For overlapping subject categories, a *see also* reference is given.